Peaks & Valleys

Overcoming Challenges and Living Your Best Life

By Paul J. Brown

Dedication

I dedicate this book to the person who just suffered a life changing injury or has been diagnosed with a serious disease and to those who continue to face their challenges with determination and a smile.

Table of Contents

Preface   6

July 4th, 1977 - Independence Day   8

Suburban Hospital, Bethesda, MD   13

Growing Up   17

Suburban Hospital, July 5th, 1977   26

Summer 1977   34

August 1977 - A Setback   37

A Turning Point   45

Late August - In Physical Therapy   49

September, Start of Senior Year Classes   51

Mid-September, Little Hoyas Football Game   53

October, Weekend Home Visit   57

Late October - Back Home   59

Senior Year, Second Semester, January 1978   63

Graduation - May 28, 1978   66

Summer 1978   69

September 1978, Mr. St. Mary's College, Freshman year72

September 1979, Sophomore year   79

Sophomore Year - Second Semester   82

September 1980, Junior year   84

September 1981, Senior year   87

Golfing Highlights   100

Beulah Beach Club 104

Dad 126

Transitions 133

Mother 135

Advanced Physical Therapy - Valerie Gibson, PT, DPT 139

Suburban Hospital, January 2012 146

Spasticity 152

Post-traumatic Tethered Spinal Cord 155

The National Institutes of Health 162

Shady Grove Adventist Rehabilitation Hospital 169

2013 188

2014 196

2015 198

Ekso Robotic: Eksoskeleton 204

2016 210

2017 218

Lessons I've learned 224

Acknowledgements 235

Man's greatest accomplishment is not in never falling but in rising again after you fall - Vince Lombardi

Preface

On Monday, July 4th, 1977, at the age of 17, I suffered a severe and life-threatening spinal cord injury diving into the shallow end of a friend's backyard swimming pool. I broke my 4th and 6th cervical vertebrae and dislocated my 5th, leaving me paralyzed from the neck down. A quadriplegic. This is the incident or accident that sadly has been a large factor in how I have had to live my life. I've tried not to let it define me.

This is a story of that night and the many other challenges I have dealt with over the last 40 years. It's an account of ups and downs or peaks and valleys, good times and not so good times. I've also written about the wonderful friends and family that have helped me through this exceptional journey. The great doctors and nurses whose skills and compassion gave me the best chance to overcome the medical challenges I've confronted. This is by no means a self-help book. It's just my story and I hope some of the things I've learned in dealing with these challenges will help you with some of the difficulties in your life. Regardless of how it may look, everyone has challenges, some bigger than others and in most cases, there is someone in a worse situation than you. Everyone is dealing with issues either personal or within their family. I look at my life and although it's not how I would have planned it, I feel at peace now and content. I've had a couple people tell me I should write a book over the last year. They've asked me questions about my injury and that leads to me telling them the story about a situation I've had to deal with. I never felt that I could write a book, but in January 2017, I started writing down one story and that led to another and after a few months, I realized I may have a book that might be interesting, helpful and possibly inspiring. I write for about 30 minutes every night in bed on my iPad. I've written every letter and word with my right thumb. It's slow but it got the job done. I hope you find it interesting and entertaining. Enjoy.

July 4th, 1977 - Independence Day

The day started out like many other July days, hot and humid. It was a Monday and a holiday, and my father was home from work, and he wanted to get some jobs done around the house. I had different plans. I had been at the eastern shore on a friend's boat all weekend and since it was a holiday, I didn't have a summer league basketball game. I was playing in Summer league games almost every weeknight, so I was planning to spend most of the day at my friend's house. My dad told me many times to cut the grass and I knew I wasn't leaving until I did. I finally finished the lawn and was in the car ready to back out of the driveway when he came to the driver's side window and asked me where I was going, that I still had work to do, I said I was done and started to back out of the driveway and before he could make another comment, he said, "You ran over my foot." I stopped the car, but he told me to go. I was late and needed to pick up my friend Shawn who lived a few blocks away from me. Then we picked up Paul and Matt, two other grade school friends and went to the house of a high school friend of mine, Kevin, who lived in Potomac Maryland and had an in-ground pool in his backyard.

I had spent many days at Kevin's house, playing tennis and swimming. The five of us had a great day. We watched the fireworks that night at Congressional Country Club a few blocks away and then we went back to Kevin's to swim. Earlier in the day we bought a few six packs of beer using a friend's fake ID and we were swimming and having a good time. Kevin's backyard pool was a rectangular pool with three steps extending out from the shallow end. There was a floating rope that divided the shallow end, 3 feet, from the deeper end of the pool which was 12 feet. Kevin could dive out over the steps and clear the rope. It had to be almost 9 feet. I was watching him do it and the competitor in me wanted to try. I went to the back of the yard got a running start and dove out over the steps aiming to clear the rope. I realized in midair that I wasn't going to be able to dive over the rope, so I ducked my head to avoid scraping my face on the rope and dove in short of the rope. I would have to try again, but I would need a longer running start.

This is the point in time that I would return to after I built a time machine and go back to July 4, 1977 at approximately 10:30 pm. Maybe I could figure out some way to trip myself and cause a sprained ankle. Oh, how different things would have been. Anyway, back to the story. I quickly jumped out of the pool, went farther back in the yard, and running as fast as my legs could go, I jumped off my right foot and again, I have the same midair realization that I was not going to clear the rope so again, like the first try I ducked my head to avoid hitting the rope. By tucking my head to my chest, it created an entry angle that sent my body down and running my head into the bottom of the pool. The impact of my head on the bottom of the pool caused a severe injury to my neck and spinal cord.

I didn't know how, but I absolutely knew I was badly injured as soon as my head hit the bottom of the pool. I knew I was in big trouble. I had a buzzing all through my body. I wasn't knocked out, I was completely conscious. I have talked to many people that have had similar injuries and most have said the same things right after their injury. After my head hit the pool bottom the force flipped me over and left me face down in the water unable to move. I tried to move my arms and my fingers to turn myself over and get a breath. Nothing. I was floating for about 20 seconds, but it seemed a lot longer than that. I never lost consciousness, but I was beginning to panic. Lucky for me, my friend Shawn Fennell, who I met in first grade and who has been one of my closest friends for the last 50 years, was there that night.

Shawn, for some reason, didn't think I was just goofing around, or playing dead man's float, quickly jumped in the water and turned me over. Saving my life.   A minute later and I would probably have drowned. He later said he could instantly see in my eyes that something was seriously wrong. He floated me to the side of the pool and he and my friends lifted me out onto the deck. Maybe moving me out of the water and onto the deck wasn't the best idea, but at the time I wanted to get out of the water. Kevin ran into the house, told his parents and his Aunt Kate, who was a nurse at Suburban Hospital and just happened to be at Kevin's house that night. She came out to check on me at the pool and quickly called 911.

I laid on the cement deck face down (that's how the guys laid me down) for what seemed like an eternity but was probably 10-15 minutes. My friends stayed close to me giving me encouragement. Telling me I was going to be ok, but I had a bad feeling. The Cabin John Fire and Rescue Squad arrived and put me on a backboard. They immobilized my neck with a cervical collar and wrapped every part of my body with ace bandages to the board to stop any additional movement that could cause additional damage. They put me on a stretcher and loaded me into the emergency vehicle where they quickly transported me from Potomac, Maryland to Suburban Hospital in Bethesda, Maryland where I was rushed into the emergency room. Shawn went back into the house and he and Kevin's dad called my dad to tell them about the accident. Then Shawn got back on the phone and explained to my dad what had happened.

Suburban Hospital, Bethesda, MD

My injury would be diagnosed that night as a hyperflexion fracture of C4 and C6 and dislocation of C5 vertebrae. The dislocation of C5 would be where the major spinal cord damage would be. Clinically, damage to the spinal cord at the C5 vertebra affects the vocal cords, biceps, and deltoid muscles in the upper arms. Unlike some of the higher cervical injuries, a patient with a C5 spinal cord injury will likely be able to breathe and speak on their own but breathing will be weak. I was a quadriplegic, also referred to as tetraplegic by definition is paralysis caused by illness or injury that results in the partial or total loss of use of all four limbs and torso; The loss is usually sensory and motor, which means that both sensation and control are lost. I was paralyzed from the neck down. I did have some sensation in my legs. I couldn't move my legs, but I could feel my legs being touched. At this point I was in a whole lot of trouble. One thing I had going for me, is that I was probably in the best shape of my life. For a month prior to the injury I had been working out, running and lifting weights while getting ready for my senior year football season. It was a good thing because I was going to be in for the fight of my life.

My parents were already in the emergency room of the hospital when I was brought in about 11:30 pm. I never asked them about that call, the phone ringing late at night, what were they thinking on the ride to the hospital not knowing how I was. It must have been terrible. But when I saw them, they were calm and assured me that I would be ok. I heard that the late-night call had woken everyone up in my house and that my mother told my older sister Christine what had happened before leaving for the hospital. Marian and Diane had heard Christine talking on the phone. She was upset explaining to the caller what had happened to me and they overheard her.

When I first arrived to the emergency room I was wearing only a wet bathing suit. Then I was moved into a room and at that point it felt like things were moving slowly but minutes later a young neurosurgeon who was on call that night, Dr. Donald Cooney, came in to see me, he introduced himself and talked to me very calmly. To test my reflexes, he took a metal instrument and rubbed it on the bottom of my foot. My foot didn't react. He used another instrument that had a metal wheel that looked like a spur. He rolled it up and down each leg and I couldn't feel it. He poked me with a pin all over my body. The only place I could feel it was on my shoulders and chest. The neck brace that the EMT's had put on me was removed and then things started moving fast. First, traction tongs were attached to the temple area of my head. They would be used for 8 weeks of cervical traction. It's a good thing I couldn't see what they were going to do because I would have been terrified. They injected my temples with lidocaine and then started screwing in the tongs that is sometimes referred to as a "halo". It was the most painful thing I had experienced in my short lifetime. I had a catheter put in and was sent for x-rays.

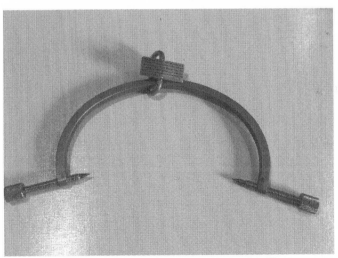

Traction Tongs "Halo"

After reviewing the X-rays, Dr. Cooney told me and my parents that the best course of action was to have surgery immediately to relieve the pressure on my spinal cord and repair the damage. That would be my best chance to get feeling and movement back. Sometime after midnight Dr. Cooney would perform a laminectomy that took over 8 hours. He wanted to open my spinal column, repair the broken vertebrae and relieve the pressure on my damaged spinal cord. I didn't need any screws or spinal fusion. Then the waiting period would begin to see if the swelling of my spinal cord would go down and hopefully, I would regain some feeling in my limbs. He told my parents that the 48 hours after surgery would be key. The next day I woke up in the ICU in a hospital bed and in traction, still paralyzed from the neck down.

Growing Up

I was born on April 14, 1960 at George Washington Hospital in Washington, DC. To this day it is still the warmest April 14th on record in DC - 94 degrees. I lived for three years on McKinley Street directly across the street from the same hospital where the Cabin John Rescue squad would bring me 17 years later. When I was three, we moved to a new house in a new development called Old Farm, located in Rockville MD. We settled into a new neighborhood where I made many friends. Most of us would attend St. Elizabeth Catholic School. Sports and competition dominated my early years. I played little league baseball, pee wee football and CYO basketball. We had a basketball hoop on our driveway. My brother Tom, who was three years older, would play 1 on 1 with me all the time. The games were usually one sided but playing against him made me a pretty good player.

Pee Wee Football - I'm #43 & Shawn is #47

Little League (bottom row, 3rd from left)

My father, Richard "Dick" Brown, was a very good football player at Gonzaga High School in the city, coached many of my teams growing up. He made sure I had the right equipment and that my uniform was worn properly. He would polish my shoes before games and oil my baseball glove. And then there were the pregame breakfasts where he would make me pancakes and bacon and eggs. Then he would drive me up to the field and as I got out of his car he would usually say "give 'em hell, Zinger," his nickname for me. Those days are burned into my mind and some of my fondest memories.

Outside of organized sports, I spent most of my free time with neighborhood friends playing football, basketball or whiffle ball until it was too dark to see. I remember my friend setting up a spotlight on a ladder in his parent's backyard, so we could play late into the night. I watched any sporting event on TV with my dad or brother, running outside during commercials to shoot a few baskets. I was a sports junkie. I was a competition junkie. I loved any game, Monopoly, Battleship, throwing crumpled up paper into a trash can. I wanted to win every game and when I didn't win, I got angry. I was a poor loser. I was cocky and a trash talker and I believe this is one of the main reasons I can deal with all the adversity I've encountered during my life. I love a challenge and I usually root for the underdog.

After graduating from St. E's in 1974, I applied to a few local Catholic high schools. I applied to Good Counsel High in Wheaton, MD, Gonzaga High in Washington, DC (where my dad went) and my first choice, Georgetown Prep in Bethesda, MD. My brother was going to be a senior there and I had spent three years going to his games, meeting the priests and teachers, and generally falling in love with the school. There was just one problem with my plan. I didn't get accepted to Prep. So, my parents and I decided that I would go to 9th grade in public school. I went to Tilden Jr. High school not far from where we lived. I knew a lot of kids from the neighborhood and had a great time there. I reapplied to Prep in the summer and was put on the waiting list. Once again, I did not get accepted for sophomore year. I was very disappointed. But because Gonzaga was so difficult to commute to, I attended Good Counsel High school in Wheaton Maryland for my sophomore year. On Friday, after my first week of classes, I was cutting grass at my neighbor's house. During the summer, I made money cutting grass for many houses in my neighborhood. My mother drove up and said she had just gotten a call from Prep admissions and she told me that I had been accepted. Of course, I still wanted to go there, so Monday morning I restarted my sophomore year at Georgetown Prep. I've wondered sometimes how different my life would have been if I never attended Prep. My sophomore year went well, I played JV football in the fall and JV basketball in the winter. Even though I was the "new" kid, I knew many of my classmates. A few I knew from my class at St. Elizabeth's and some others through years of playing CYO basketball.

Prep Varsity Football - Junior Year

In the Spring '77, I got the opportunity to travel with other high school students to France for 10 days.

It was a great trip, traveling around the French countryside. We visited many cities, traveling in a bus 3-4 hours each day. We sampled the French food and wine. There wasn't any drinking age, so we took advantage of that. We saw a great deal of the country. One day was spent at Mont Saint Michel, and another at Normandy Beach. The last three days in Paris, we saw The Louvre and other iconic places and I walked to the very top of the Eiffel Tower. It was a fun trip, but I was very glad to get home. I missed the food back at home, my friends and my family. My mother was so smart to have me go.

During the summer I worked at Pete's Pizza and Sub Shop. My dad had his own coffee business and Pete's was one of his customers. Pete's was in the Rockville Mall. I worked there during the weekdays and continued my small grass cutting business in the evenings and weekends. Any other time was spent with my friends playing basketball or hanging out at the neighborhood pool. I attended the Prep summer football camp for two weeks in August. We stayed in the dorms on campus. It was tough during the hot summer days with 2 practices in the day. At night we played cards and listened to music. Anyone who was going to play on the JV or varsity teams attended the camp. I was fortunate to make the varsity team. We had a great season and only lost 1 game and finished ranked #3 in the Washington Post rankings. Like many athletes, I enjoyed the camaraderie of team sports. The competitive aspect is important, but the friendships developed and being part of a team are valuable later in life. I also made the varsity basketball team which also had a very successful season too. Our team will be inducted to Georgetown Prep's Hall of Fame in the Spring of 2019. I played golf in the Spring and went to the prom in May. My junior year at Prep was over and I was looking forward to Summer. I knew I was going to be working, cutting grass and taking a summer school French class (flunked) but I also planned to get into better shape.

Varsity Basketball - Junior year

One of my goals for my senior year was to get some more playing time on the varsity football team. I spent my junior year on the bench, although I had an interception in our last game getting garbage time in a blowout against Central High School. I only got on the field when we were way ahead. I was also playing summer league basketball almost every night in DC or Maryland I played on the varsity basketball team but rode the bench. But that talented senior class had graduated in the Spring, and I felt I could get more playing time in my senior year. I was back to cutting grass to make money and spent weekends with my close grade school friends. I was working out after work and on the weekends and was in good shape. If I only knew about what lay ahead of me, maybe it was better I didn't.

Suburban Hospital, July 5th, 1977

I woke up the next morning in a regular hospital bed in the Intensive Care Unit. The other beds used for patients needing spinal traction were being used so they had to make do with a regular bed. My head was halfway hanging off the top of the mattress with a makeshift traction apparatus connected to my traction tongs. I spent a little more than two days like this while the hospital tried to find a suitable bed. Lying in this position for that long would be very detrimental to my health. During that short time, I developed bed sores on my heels and tailbone, and a large bedsore on the back of my head. They would become a very serious medical problem. The edge of the bed combined with the pull of the weights had worn a 4" diameter bedsore on the back of my head in less than two days.

While I was in intensive care, my family could visit me for only 10 minutes every hour. I remember how noisy it was in there and that most of the time the overhead lights were on and the machines were beeping. There weren't many private rooms, just beds divided by curtains. It was supposed to be a temporary stop. I was only in the ICU for a few days until I had recovered from the surgery and to make sure that I wasn't having any breathing issues which can happen with spinal cord injured patients.

When my two younger sisters, Marian and Diane saw me, I think they were a little shocked. But who wouldn't be? Lots of tubes and wires connected to their brother who had looked much different days earlier. Because you had to be 16 years old to go into the ICU, they had to dress like they were older. When they came in, I was very sedated and had no idea what I looked like. They didn't stay long, they just wanted to see me and say hi. I'm sure like most people at that early stage, they weren't too sure what had happened to me and just what my future would hold. Neither did I.

Today when I visit with people in the hospital, I'm a little uncomfortable too, maybe like most people. I make small talk with the person and offer some encouragement but in the back of my mind I'm glad that's not me in that bed. I make a better patient than a visitor. Probably because I've had so much experience.

Eventually, the hospital was finally able to acquire a Navy Stryker frame bed a few days later from the National Institutes of Health just across the street. The bed reminded me of the frame or stretcher they use to rescue injured hikers on the side of a mountain. I believe it was used in military hospitals. I would spend the next 8 weeks in that bed. To avoid further bedsores, the plan would be that I would be turned over every 2 hours 24/7. At least that was what was supposed to happen. For two hours I would lie flat on a stretcher type frame with a mattress made of foam which got hot. I was wearing a hospital gown. I had a catheter and attached to my head tongs was a cord with weights hanging off the Stryker frame. When I was face up, I was looking at the ceiling and anywhere else that my eyes could move. I couldn't turn my head left or right because of the traction. When I visited with people, they had to stand directly over me, so I could see their face. I watched TV on an 8-inch black and white beauty. But it was better than the alternative. At the end of the 2-hour period, which I would try to stretch as long as possible, I would be flipped over. Then my view was of the linoleum hospital floor. Sometimes my brother and sisters and friends would lie down on the floor on a beach towel, so I could see and talk to them.

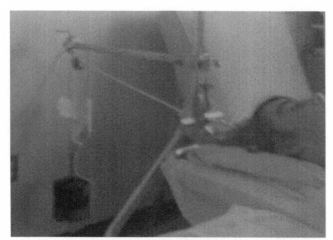

Traction Weights

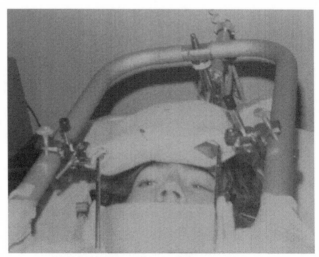

Navy Stryker Frame

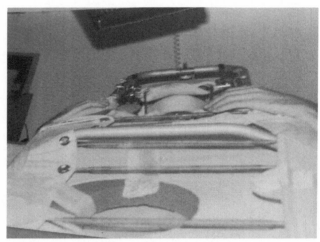

Sandwiched in my "Bed" ready to be flipped

An identical bed frame with a hole for my face (like on a massage table) would be placed on top of me "secured" with a screw at each end and then I would be quickly turned over now facing the hospital tile floor. Many times, if I was not turned quickly enough, I would fall out of the side of the frames and onto the floor only connected to the bed by my tongs and traction weights. As I learned the key was to flip the bed fast, but the staff turned me too slow probably not wanting to damage my neck. In my first of many "work arounds" I asked them to wrap straps around the entire frame to keep me from falling out of the side during the flip and that worked. But as many times as I instructed and later begged new hospital staff on how to quickly flip the bed and use the straps, I was ignored and then apologized to as I was picked up off the floor still attached to the bed by the weights, a rope and my tongs.

I spent eight long weeks in that bed while the bones in my neck were healing. Now spinal cord injured patients are fitted with a "halo vest". This technique is based on the attachment of the halo to a device worn around the patient's torso, rather than equipment attached to a hospital bed, to provide the needed force to immobilize the cervical spine. The modern version of the halo vest attaches through adjustable metal bars to a rigid, lightweight, fleece-lined vest that fits snugly about the patient's chest. This apparatus provides continuous stability to the cervical spine while simultaneously allowing the patient to be comfortable and mobile. The advantages of the vest include precise positional control and solid external stabilization of the cervical spine, ease of application, a low complication rate, minimal patient discomfort, and early patient mobilization. The halo vest has been shown to be extremely effective at preventing further neurological injury for patients who have sustained cervical spinal injuries. Studies have demonstrated excellent rates of healing after three months of halo vest use however, that was not an option for me in 1977.

My days in that "bed" were long. There wasn't much to do. I spent most days watching TV. Because I could only see straight up and down, my brother figured out a way to prop a stick in the top of the TV and tilt it down, so I could watch. It only had a small screen, but it was an asset for passing the hours and I could only see the TV when I was on my back. I can remember watching The Price is Right, Family Feud, and in the afternoon watching The Gong Show. My mother watched the soap opera All My Children every day at 1 o'clock and soon I was hooked. I had a small transistor radio playing the top 40 songs and to this day I remember a song I would hear all the time. It was a song by Stephen Bishop called "On and On". The lyrics were profound. "On and on he just keeps on trying and he smiles when he feels like dying, on and on, on and on, on and on".

Friends of mine would visit, which would give my family a break and we re-established our old Friday night poker games that we had played in grade school and high school. I would be face down and we would deal the cards on the floor. Put our money in the pot on the floor and have many laughs. These visits were so important to me. It was a wonderful break from all the monotony. There were days when my mental outlook was positive, and it would last for a few days. Then maybe a bad night or some small disappointment would change my mood for the worst. It wasn't too hard to tell from looking at me or my lack of conversation how I was feeling. My dad was sitting with me after dinner one night after one of those bad days and he said" Zinger, in life there are peaks and valleys and even though things are bad today, just focus on tomorrow and it will be a better day". I hear his voice saying that when things get tough.

I didn't realize at the time but on my chart, there was a place for religion and since I was Catholic, from time to time a priest would visit me in my room. What started out as a nice gesture over time became a little annoying. It seemed like the priest would show up at the worst times: either I was asleep or just wanted to be alone or eating a meal. I know they meant well but eventually I asked my mother to stop the visits. One of the last priests to visit was the pastor of our church Fr. Bloom. He told me that because I was suffering now, I wouldn't have any suffering in the future. That sounded good to me at the time. I did think for years after my injury that I had more than paid my dues and that certainly nothing this bad would ever happen to me again. Now that's textbook foreshadowing.

Summer 1977

My mother would come to the hospital around eight o'clock every morning after dropping Diane off at school. She was still taking care of the house, making sure my younger sisters were doing what they were supposed to do at home and in school. Tom was in college and Christine was just starting her career in mortgage banking. My mother was under tremendous stress, but when she was with me, she was always positive. I don't think I ever saw her when she wasn't upbeat. She knew when to push me and when I needed a break. When she arrived in the morning, she would get a report of how my night was from the nurse's station. It was rare that my nights were ever good. After my friends and family had gone home, usually after visiting hours, I was alone. I put on a tough exterior during the day, but the nights were long and very difficult. One of the things that I can't forget is that many nights phlebotomists would come to draw blood. They came late in the evening or even in the middle of the night. Like most people I don't like needles and hated getting my blood taken. I could hear the test tubes rattling in their carts. Were they coming for me or my roommate or were they just passing by my door? It would keep me up for an hour until I was sure they were gone. I referred to them as vampires.

The night shift of nurses was usually ok, but occasionally, I would get a nurse that probably should have been in another line of work. I was in pain, but it would take them what seemed like forever to bring my pain medication. I wouldn't get turned over on time and sometimes I would end up on the floor. I would scream at them. All I had to defend myself was my voice, my words. I couldn't move, I couldn't punch or grab. I couldn't scratch my nose or shoo a fly off me. So, most mornings my mom would get a report on me and the file would read "patient belligerent". Damn right I was. I wasn't giving in, I was going to fight and scrap and cuss and not accept my bad situation. I feel like I've been doing that for most of my life. No, things don't always go my way, but I do the best I can and move on. Looking back, I have no idea how I was able to get through those tough days. I had none of the "tricks of the trade" or the experience I now have dealing with adversity. The knowledge of how to survive long days and nights in a hospital. How to deal with pain and depression. I was just dealing with each situation as it came, one by one, but not alone. The medical staff, my parents, my brother, my sisters and friends and me working as a team trying to make the best of a bad situation. I was only 17 but growing up fast. I had no other option.

One of the benefits of being so young was not knowing how bad my situation was regarding my injury and prognosis. I remember thinking that summer football camp didn't start for 5 weeks so I certainly could be ready for that. I'd broken bones before. This was just another injury, although a bit more serious. I had been hurt before, broke my knee in a football game. You put a cast on it and eight weeks later you were running around again. Well of course the doctors and my parents knew how bad my injury and prognosis were and they intentionally kept it from me. A smart decision. It wasn't that they didn't answer my questions if I asked. They just put a positive spin on the answer. So, I don't remember being that afraid. I felt like I was dealing with everything that was being thrown at me but apparently my body was not handling the stress.

August 1977 - A Setback

Approximately four weeks after my injury, I started to lose a lot of blood. One day I was feeling ok and the next day I was in serious trouble. Due to the bleeding, my doctor thought I had an ulcer somewhere in my digestive system. A stress ulcer is not uncommon for this type of injury. Over a three-day period, I was given 12 pints of blood. I was moved back to ICU and a nasogastric tube (NG) was inserted through my nose into my stomach. For 24 hours a nurse pumped ice water through the tube and removed it hoping that would stop the bleeding. She repeated the process over and over. But it didn't work. The bleeding continued, and blood transfusions were continued, but my health was slowly deteriorating. I was taken to an operating room for further diagnosis. At this time, I was still in a halo, which was attached to my temporal area with two screws. A rope was attached to a hook at the top of the halo and weights hung off a rod at the end of my Stryker frame. To be moved to the surgical table and out of my "bed" the traction on my cervical spine had to be done manually. Dr. Cooney held my halo and manually kept the proper amount of traction on my cervical spine while the surgeon performed an angiogram hoping to find the source of the bleeding. He spent at least an hour trying to find the source of the bleeding, but he didn't find it. Had they found a problem, I would have stayed there for surgery to fix the problem.

For some unknown reason the bleeding seemed to have stopped and they didn't have to do any surgery. I was awake while all this was going on. I was very scared and barely holding it together. After the angiogram was completed, they closed the incision in my groin. Dr. Cooney wanted to do a spinal tap (to check for blood in my spinal cord) while I was in the OR. He asked me how I was doing, I lied and told him I was okay. He did the tap and the pain was unbearable I couldn't move my legs and my sensation was minimal, but I could sure feel the needle. When he finally finished, I threw up and I felt a little better. After getting the results back from the lab, he told my parents that not only has the internal bleeding stopped but also there wasn't any blood in my spinal fluid. That was very important for my recovery. The surgery to repair the break and dislocation in my cervical spine was a success but my paralysis was most likely permanent.

My parents visited me after I was brought back to the ICU and gave me the good news. It was very late, and I was completely wiped out. I was crying because I was told they were going to start the ice water again for another day to make sure the bleeding had stopped. They needed to insert another NG tube. I couldn't take any more. My mother had to be feeling terrible, but she didn't patronize me. She treated me like an adult because after all I'd been through those last few weeks, I wasn't a kid anymore. She knew it had to be done. So, in the early morning in the ICU she looked me in the eyes and said, "I know you can do it" and I believed her.

The next morning, no more bleeding, no one knew why, and it didn't really matter. I was moved back to my room. Around this time, the hospital's doctors were telling my parents that after I got out of traction, I should be transferred to a rehab hospital in Baltimore, MD. They were more equipped to treat and rehab spinal cord injuries. But my mother believed that I should stay at Suburban and be closer to home and friends and family. She believed it was just as important for me to have my friends and family visit to keep my spirits up. She convinced my doctor to let me stay.

From the first day I was admitted my mother came to the hospital just about every day. She was usually there from 8am to 3pm. My dad came in around 5 pm after he finished working and stayed until after dinner. He would leave if I had visitors or stay until I went to sleep. At that point hospital visiting hours didn't pertain to me. I was something of a celebrity. My brother and sisters visited often. My older sister Christine (23) was working. My brother Tom (20) was between his sophomore and junior year at Mt. St. Mary's College. My sisters Marian (14) just about to start high school and Diane (13) was going into the 8th grade. Other visitors like my Uncle Chick and Uncle JB visited often. I had pain in my jaw probably from the Stryker frame face mask and luckily my Uncle Chick was my dentist and helped adjust the mask and alleviate the pain. It seemed there was always something to deal with.

The next four weeks were much of the same. I was back in a regular hospital room and I was getting visitors every day and receiving get well cards from my friends, classmates, aunts and uncles. My room was covered with cards and get-well posters and stuffed animals. It looked like I had been there a long time, because I had. My Nana and Papa (Dad's parents) who lived in Florida, sent a card almost every day with my grandfather writing a terribly corny joke in each one. They were a highlight of each day. I was getting cards from everyone and visitors brought food and if I couldn't eat it the nurses would. I got long letters from priests and prayer cards from around the country. Word of my injury and recovery had spread and everyone wanted to help. Some players on the football team donated blood to help the blood bank. The families in the neighborhood brought dinners to my house and I was curious as to what my family was eating on any given night. Because I was flat on my back, I couldn't see much of anything around me. Christine drew for me the layout of the floor, where my room was located, the elevators and the nurse's station. That gave me some perspective of my location. I was getting to know the nurses on my floor, and it was nice to have them around if my family wasn't there.

Since day one, I was in pain most of the time. Most of the pain was coming from the tongs in my head. A few times a week Dr. Cooney had to tighten the screws on each side to make sure they were functioning properly. I was getting injections of Demerol once or twice a day to ease the pain. As the weeks went by, I was dealing with the pain or building up a pain tolerance, so I was trying to cut back on the pain meds. I had also tried a rudimentary version of self-hypnosis to alleviate my pain. I can't remember how I heard about it or where I learned about it. If I was alone and I could calm my breathing I would focus on the pain, keep focusing on the area of the pain and after a few minutes the pain signal would seem to dissipate. It would help for 30-60 minutes. I wasn't sure what I was doing but it helped and that's all that mattered to me. It would get me to the time for my next injection.

It seemed that as soon as my situation stabilized a little, I got thrown a curveball. Two weeks after my bleeding ulcer, I was losing my appetite and losing weight. The doctors later figured out I had developed a form of hepatitis from the 12 blood transfusions. I was given drugs but as weeks went by dealing with this, my weight got as low as 100 pounds before the medication eventually worked. I would eventually recover. I was trying to eat and put the weight back on but couldn't because I had no appetite. People were bringing me milkshakes and doughnuts, anything they thought I might like but nothing appealed to me. One day my dad brought chicken wings from a local restaurant in town (Manny's) and I loved them. I was finally getting my appetite back. He told the bar owner that I was eating his wings and he gave my dad a big box of wings for me every night. I eventually got tired of the wings, but the nurses loved them. This was just another complication from my injury and at that time I was very lucky to recover from it.

I was starting to get better physically. I was putting some weight back on. The paralysis was bad enough, but the complications from the spinal cord injury were becoming the biggest problem. I was fighting these issues one by one and hadn't started any rehab. The one issue that was not going away was the bed sore on my tailbone. It was not healing like the other ones, in fact it was getting worse. A plastic surgeon was brought in and he was trying to avoid having to do a skin graft by trying less aggressive treatments. I was spending more time face down to help the problem, which I hated. They tried different types of mattresses to keep the pressure off my tailbone. Eventually, many weeks later the sore finally healed on its own. But it turned out to be the main reason I couldn't be released from the hospital for months.

It was the middle of August and not surprising I wouldn't be going to Prep's football camp; but very soon I would get the tongs removed and then I could start rehab. I got movement back in my shoulders and arms. My hands and fingers were slower to recover but I was making progress. At that time, I had to be fed all meals. I was eating lying flat on my back which wasn't easy. It was becoming very frustrating to rely on people to do everything for me. Feed me, bathe me, dress me. It was humbling and sometimes humiliating. I went without when I didn't want to bother someone. I hated being a burden. But I had to adjust to my new life, and it was important to ask for help. Today, I'm still adjusting to everyday challenges. When I find a "fix" for a problem eventually a new one will pop up. I never get used to it and I've had 40 years of experience, but I must keep on going and not get upset. The one thing even to this day that I have difficulty with is when my life seems to be going well in the back of my mind I am wondering when the next setback or problem is going to confront me. I try to keep those thoughts to a minimum but it's not easy.

A Turning Point

I was frustrated as to why I hadn't gotten any movement back in my legs. Not knowing my prognosis, I believed my paralysis was just temporary, nobody had told me differently. Dr. Cooney tested my leg muscles when he visited which was just about every day. He asked me to push or resist against him and I couldn't. I did have some skin sensation. For example, I could tell if someone was touching my left foot or right foot. My left arm and hand were getting a little better. The movement in my right hand and fingers was slower to improve. It is not uncommon with this type of injury to have one side of the body be more affected. The exam ended after he tested my arm strength. He checked my traction and answered any questions I had. Usually one of my parents talked with him outside my room after each visit. I knew they were concerned that my condition wasn't getting better but probably not that surprised. Still everyone was hoping that I would be able to walk again.

At night when I was on my stomach, I visualized moving my toe. I use visualization techniques in my therapy to this day. I've read a few articles on the subject and I think it helps me. I was told that the key to me walking again is to move my toes. That would mean that some of the motor nerve connections were not damaged. I had a feeling at night when all was quiet and if I concentrated, that I could move my toe, but it could have been just my imagination. Also, my Great Aunt Alice had given me a pair of prism glasses so when lying down I could see my toes when I tried to move them. I told the nurse in the morning and we tried to recreate it during the day. I would wear the glasses and the nurse or whoever was there would say to move my toes and I would try. With an injury like this, I would have involuntary spasms, so I must move my toe when I am asked to. I was sure I was moving my toe at night, but I was unable to prove it during the day. It became an exercise I tried with anyone who was in my room. I was thinking everyone was just going along with it for my benefit, but I was sure I wasn't imagining it. I had this feeling, a confidence that I would be able to walk again.

Then one morning, my brother Tom and sister Marian were visiting. Like most mornings I asked him, or whoever was there, to watch my toe. I was going to try again. I closed my eyes, concentrated and he said" move your toes" and I thought my left big toe moved. Nothing was said. He said, "try it again" and it moved again. He said, "you're moving your left big toe." I knew it! He got the nurse to show her. I moved it again and for the rest of that morning people came to my room to see the show. My brother came back in the room and said, "I've done my miracle for today so I'm going home." News spread around the hospital and some people are using the "miracle" word. I wasn't sure about that, but it was a great day. My mother watched me move my toe and was ecstatic. We got word to my dad and my family. I showed Dr. Cooney and a big smile was on his face. That was a big show of emotion from the stoic doctor. What I believed was happening was that when I was moving my toe at night, I had exhausted my toe muscle. When I tried to show someone the next day it wouldn't move. Anyway, that was what we'd all been hoping for. I had a chance to get better.

A week later it was finally time to get out of the Stryker frame and most importantly that damn traction halo. It had been 8 weeks and my cervical vertebrae had healed. In the early morning of July 5, Donald Cooney, who was on call for the resident neurosurgeon, Dr. Lord, performed a posterior cervical laminectomy to relieve pressure on the spinal cord caused by my diving injury. So late August with my mother watching Dr. Cooney, removed the traction weights and began unscrewing the tongs from my head. Over the eight weeks of traction, the bone and tissue in my skull had adhered to the screws, and I was glad he didn't tell me it was going to hurt as much coming out as it did going in.

I was finally free and was transferred to a regular hospital bed. I could raise the bed slightly and could start physical therapy soon and after 8 weeks I was finally able to wash my hair which I was looking forward to. I was fitted with a neck brace, not the big foamy kind. It was a two-piece metal contraption that fit on my back and chest with a cradle under my chin. It was very uncomfortable to move in and to sleep in, but it beat the hell out of the traction tongs.

Finally up in a wheelchair with Marian and Diane.

Late August - In Physical Therapy

Therapists came to my room the next morning and began moving my legs. They set up a pulley system over my new bed to exercise my arms. I would be able to go down to therapy soon. I had to start trying to sit up by raising the head of my bed up a little more each day. A couple of days later I was transferred from my bed to a wheelchair and immediately I was light headed. The therapy tech tilted me back before I passed out. For 8 weeks I had been completely horizontal. Any time I raised my head up more than a few inches my blood pressure dropped, and I felt like I was going to pass out and sometimes I did. When I finally was able to get to the therapy room I began to work on a head-up tilt table. The primary use of the tilt table was to transitionally bring a patient into a progressively upright standing position. They are used with bedridden, wheelchair bound patients or with people who are unable to support their own weight due to neurological impairment or injury.

There is no easy or fast way to do this. You must build up a tolerance and get your blood pressure to regulate as you get vertical. You are secured to the table and your head is lifted 15-30 degrees and you work over and over until you can tolerate sitting. During the process your blood pressure is monitored. I can remember having a lot of headaches. With spinal cord injuries the autonomic nervous system is affected. Even today my normal blood pressure is approximately 82 over 60. My body has learned to adjust to this low BP over the years and many other effects from the injury. It's amazing how a person's body can adapt to injury and physical trauma. Eventually I conquered the tilt table and settled into using a wheelchair. I would get more from my therapy sessions with more mobility and spend more time out of my room.

I remember one day in my chair I was wheeling myself up and down the hall strengthening my arms. The therapy room was right next to the front door of the hospital, so I wheeled myself right out the door into a warm rainy afternoon. It was the first time I had been outside since I was admitted. It felt incredible just to sit there by myself in the rain. Eventually the therapy tech found me and wheeled me back into the hospital. Being able to use a wheelchair allowed me to get outside and one afternoon my mother brought our dog for a visit. It was small things like that that got me through each day.

September, Start of Senior Year Classes

I was supposed to begin my senior year at Georgetown Prep in September 1977. Due to my injury most people thought that I would have to miss a year of school. I was determined to do everything I could to graduate with my class. My parents reluctantly agreed to let me have tutors in Math and English to keep me caught with up my class in school. They were hesitant to add any more stress than I already had but agreed to let me try. Tutors from Montgomery County were hired, to keep me up with my class work. So, starting in early September my morning schedule was breakfast then physical therapy followed by the math tutor then lunch. The afternoon was physical therapy then the English tutor. I usually took a nap and then had dinner. I stuck as close to this schedule as I could. But it wasn't easy. Some days I couldn't handle it physically and some days I was just mentally done. Today I'm better at handling bad days and adversity but back then dealing with the injury and all the side effects as a 17-year-old, I'm not sure how I survived it. I tried to deal with one thing at a time and focus on getting past it, but it didn't always work.

Another interesting part of a long hospital stay is your roommates. Other than my two weeks in intensive care I spent the rest of my hospital days in a two-person room. Being one of the longest-term patients at Suburban Hospital I usually had the bed by the window in all of my rooms. The other bed was a revolving door of people. Some roommates were there a week or two, some with serious illnesses or injury. I did have one man who died in the middle of the night. Most of my roommates were there for surgery the next morning or were recovering from surgery that day. I recall one guy who was in for some internal procedure making a few trips to the bathroom to smoke pot. Another was this big biker guy, shaved head and tattoos. He was in for knee surgery the next morning after crashing on his motorcycle. Late that night after all his friends had gone home, I heard him crying. He was so scared. I gave him the typical "don't worry everything will be ok" but it was funny.

Mid-September, Little Hoyas Football Game

The weekends were long and monotonous. No scheduled therapy or much else to do. I had more visitors on the weekend and most of the time I was happy to see them. Other times I wasn't in the mood for guests, but I tried to put a smile on my face. There wasn't much on TV back then. Just a few channels and not many good shows. I was getting restless. I had been in the hospital for over 2 months. The bedsore on my tailbone wasn't getting better or worse. The football season had started, and I could take a day trip to my high school to watch a home game. Prior to the start of the season, our head coach Jim Fegan visited me in the hospital. Mr. Fegan was Prep's head coach for 36 seasons, racking up an eye-popping 236 wins and capturing 14 league championships. He was inducted into the State of Maryland High School Football Hall of Fame and the DC Touchdown Club "Circle of Legends". We had a nice visit and before leaving, he assured me I was still part of the team and asked me what jersey number I wanted. It was a wonderful gesture and I chose the number 40.

On game day, I put my jersey on over my neck and body brace and was transferred from my wheelchair into the front seat of my mother's new dove grey Thunderbird to see the Georgetown Prep Little Hoyas play. The school had arranged it so we could drive the car behind the end zone area, so I could watch from the car. It was great to be out of the hospital. Many friends and students visited me at my car during the game. We won the game and just when we were getting ready to leave the entire team ran towards the car. They surrounded the car cheering loudly. Then the team captains gave me the game ball. It was a day I'll always remember.

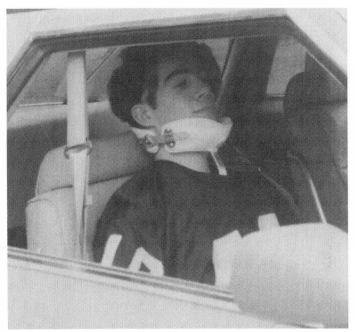
Watching the "Little Hoyas" from the car

We drove back to the hospital. Seeing everyone from school was just the lift I needed. I've learned how important the non-physical part of rehabilitation is. You need to have drive and motivation and a positive outlook, or you'll never want to improve physically. I went back to my rehab on Monday, it was early October. The next Saturday I made another trip to a football game at Woodbridge High School where we beat a very talented Virginia public school team. I think they had more people in their band then we had in our entire school, which was a little over 300.

My rehab was going well but I wasn't getting the improvement in my legs that I would need to stand, let alone walk again.   Dr. Henry Scruggs was the doctor in charge of my case. He had been my general practitioner since I left my pediatrician. He was a close friend of my parents and our neighbor and the father of my grade school friend, Kitty. Looking back on my time dealing with this injury, my parents and I were very lucky to have Dr. Scruggs' support. He worked with my parents, got me the best doctors available and made my "adventure" at Suburban Hospital as good as possible. He allowed me to bypass some of the hospital rules which really helped me get through my long stay.

October, Weekend Home Visit

On Friday, October 20th, Dr. Scruggs said it would be ok to go home for the weekend. I would be able to sleep at home for two nights. My father quickly built a ramp for my eventual return home so that I could get my wheelchair into the front door of my house on Farmland Drive. They moved the furniture out of the dining room and set up a bed. It was just a weekend, but it was a pretty big deal for all of us. I arrived home Friday afternoon and can still remember how happy our dog was to see me. Our dog was named Dog, the reason for that is a story for another time. I enjoyed the weekend being home, watching college football on Saturday, eating home cooked meals, but in the back of my mind, I knew I would have to go back to the hospital. The only thing keeping me there was the damn bedsore on my tailbone. It was just about healed but the dermatologist thought it needed more professional treatment. Then on Sunday morning the phone rang, and my mother handed me the phone and it was Dr. Scruggs and he said how would you like to stay home for good. He had gotten me my release. On October 22nd, my 110 days in the hospital were over!! I had imagined a big hospital send off as I was wheeled out to the car with cheers and balloons but that never happened, and it didn't bother me either. I was a little sad that I couldn't thank the nursing staff when I left but I would see some of the emergency room staff, for another little adventure, a few years later.

Late October - Back Home

The next six weeks at home were a big adjustment period. It was great to be home but there were obviously some things hospitals are more equipped to handle. My mother and I managed my care and figured out bathroom and bathing issues. I had a physical therapist come to my house as well as my Math and English tutors to keep me up to date with my classes. When I left the hospital, I still couldn't stand, but through hard work in physical therapy, my legs were getting stronger and eventually I was able to stand at home with support from my therapist and a walker. Once I started to stand my overall physical strength improved rapidly. By Thanksgiving I was standing using a crutch to support my weaker right side. With help I was able to take a few small steps and then I would sit in the wheelchair and rest; then a few more steps. Then the athlete in me took over. When the therapist was there, we would walk and when he wasn't there, my dad would walk holding on to me. The more I walked, the stronger I got. I could see improvement from day to day. I remember walking from one end of our kitchen to the other by myself for the first time. My dad was waiting at the other end. It was a very emotional walk for both of us. After that I would make a loop around my house through the den, front hallway then the living room, back through the dining room and kitchen and would return to a chair in the family room. I would watch TV for 15 or 20 minutes and then make another loop with a big crutch under my right arm stepping with my left leg and struggling to lift my right leg. It wasn't pretty, but I was walking. I continued to work on strengthening my arms and to work on my writing skills. My right hand was recovering slowly. I had some grip strength, but my dexterity was poor. I had to practice writing as much as possible. I had to learn to hold a pen differently but eventually after months of work my penmanship was passable. I had learned to write again.

Looking back, I'm not sure what was happening in my recovery. It was like my legs were finally waking up. The nerve connections were working again. I know this doesn't make sense and I really can't explain it. In December I was walking with a cane, but I still had a limp with my right leg. I passed my Math and English classes and was cleared to return to school in January for my last semester at Prep. My parents talked with the school's headmaster and they were willing to help me with anything I needed. I enjoyed the Christmas holidays and continued working with my therapist at home. I was able to carefully walk upstairs to my own bedroom and we had dinner back in our reclaimed dining room. Things were getting as close to normal as they had been in a long time. I remember my sister Christine giving me a Christmas card with Tiny Tim and his crutch on the front with the caption "God bless us everyone". It was funny. It was also great that we could laugh, after all we had been through. We certainly had a lot to be thankful for. We were all sitting around the dinner table including my grandmother and Great Aunt Alice. It was perfect.

Due to obviously more important issues I was dealing with since the summer, I was unable to work on my college applications. For us to even think that I would be going to college in September was silly. I obviously hadn't had time to visit any colleges or finish filling out any applications. I was able to keep up with my classes which was my priority. I also hadn't taken my SATs. A neighborhood friend of my parents, Dick Ridgeway, had offered to help. He was the father of one of my grade school classmates Dana and had coached me in CYO basketball. Mr. Ridge-way had a close relationship with the Mt. St. Mary's board of directors. I had applied for admission to the Mount because my brother was a student there and from enjoying my trips to visit him. I liked the school. Mt. St. Mary's is a small (approximately 1600 students) liberal arts college, which is now a university, and is in Emmitsburg, MD., about an hour from my house in Rockville. He told us that if I could take my SAT's, the Mount would consider my application. On a Saturday in mid-January, I somehow sat for 3 hours and took the test. My application was submitted. It would be the only college that I applied to.

Senior Year, Second Semester, January 1978

I returned to Prep in mid-January after the Christmas break. I put on my jacket and tie (required dress code) picked up my cane and headed to campus. Everyone was glad I was back but very quickly it was back to school work. I was treated the same as everyone else except I was given the elevator key in the classroom building which made me very popular. I made my way around campus and attended all my classes. My life was pretty much back to normal. In mid-February I was very happy to hear that I had been accepted to Mt. St. Mary's College. My friend Shawn, the same friend who pulled me out of the pool seven months earlier, would also be going to the Mount.

In May our class honored a long-time tradition of having a Senior skip day. We were forewarned by the administration that doing so could cause the cancellation of our prom and may jeopardize our graduation festivities. Of course, we ignored the threats and on a nice weekday in early May almost every student in our class (83 total) headed to a

Bethesda park. Being that I had turned 18 in April, I went with a couple of friends to Belby's liquor store in Rockville and we bought 2 kegs. The day was a success; music, pickup basketball games, and throwing the frisbee. When we returned to school the next day, we were given 2 days of JUG (Justice Under God) commonly known as detention, for every class we missed. A few of our more influential parents, informed the school that the prom, graduation and everything associated with graduation would happen as scheduled. One of the benefits of my detention (8 afternoons) was that I got my English term paper finished. I wrote about spinal cord injuries and their effects and physical therapy. I got a C. I was shocked. I had written my paper on spinal cord injuries and their treatment, complete with personally drawn illustrations. The ultimate irony was that months later my English teacher suffered a broken neck while jogging. Luckily, her injuries weren't as severe as mine and she made a full recovery.

Later that month I attended my senior prom. My date was coach Fagan's daughter Linda. She would also be attending the Mount in the fall. Our prom was held at the Kennedy Center. I wore all white with a top hat and tails. I painted my cane white to match my tux. I drove my mother's Thunderbird with my friend Kevin and his date. It was a fun night.

Senior Prom

Graduation - May 28, 1978

My graduation was a big day. My family was all there, including my Great Aunt Alice and my grandmother. They held graduation outdoors in the quad on Prep's campus. They called my name and I walked across the stage to get my diploma without my cane. I have a picture of me receiving my diploma, but I don't remember being on stage. The only thing I was focused on was not tripping and falling. They gave out all the remaining individual student awards and just when I thought the ceremony was about to end, the Headmaster, Fr. Sauter, said they had one more award to give out, then he started to read the following:

> It happens rarely, but occasionally, that the life and actions of a student are such that they need to be specially recognized. There is such a person among our graduates today. Last July fourth Paul Brown broke his neck while swimming. For many weeks no one knew if he would walk again. Yet, the feeling of every person who visited him was one of admiration and respect for him as each of us experienced

his joy, his hope, his determination not to allow his injury to overcome his outlook on life or his personal disposition. Most of us left Paul knowing that no obstacle was so big that it could not be lived with. Many of us walked away with a greater determination to accept the difficulties which were in our own lives, and to use them as a means of bringing ourselves and our world closer to God the Father. We therefore wish to recognize Paul in a special way today by pointing him out to all here present and awarding him the President's Medal for the example and inspiration he has given the Prep community in accepting and responding to the accident in his life in a courageous, Christian manner. - 27 May 1978

As everyone started clapping, I went back up on stage to accept the President's Medal. After the class pictures and before leaving for the graduation parties, I gave the medal to my mother. She had more than earned it.

Graduation Day with my grandmother

Summer 1978

My long and tumultuous high school journey was over. I was looking forward to the summer and starting college in September. On Saturday, July 8, 1978, my parents and I hosted a one-year anniversary party at our home in Rockville. I invited my friends, neighbors, relatives and many of the nurses and doctors from the hospital. I invited Dr. Cooney and he came with his wife. It started in the afternoon and went late into the night. It was a celebration of a successful year and a thank you to the many people who helped me and my family through the difficult challenges we faced in the past year. This anniversary party would continue annually for over 30 years to become a summer party at local hotels and finish as The Summer Bash at my current home in Vienna, Virginia.

In August of 1978, I began a series of plastic surgeries to repair the bald spot on the back of my head. The bedsore that I had gotten in the first two days in the hospital had left approximately a four-inch round patch of dead (scar tissue) skin. Each surgery would cut out a couple of inches in the center of the scarred area and the two healthy sides of scalp would be sutured tightly together making the bald patch smaller. This surgical procedure was performed by the same plastic surgeon who fixed my bedsore on my tailbone. It wasn't a walk in the park. My mother took me to his office, and I would lay face down on a padded table. Then he would start injecting the area with lidocaine over and over and over until finally it would be numb. Then he started cutting out a big piece of scar tissue. He was asking me about how my summer was going, and blood was running down the sides of my face and he was cauterizing the bleeding and chatting away. He finished by stitching the two sides together and he had to pull hard to get the two sides to meet. It took about 90 minutes. We went home with pain medication, but I felt great for a couple of hours. My mother asked me a few times if I needed any medicine. I said no because I felt fine. And then the pain hit me like a freight train. The 45 minutes for those painkillers to work were agonizing. I would have this surgery every six months or so (usually the summer and Christmas holidays) after the skin on my head became loose again. Each time the surgeon would cut out the middle, pull it together until the two healthy pieces of non-scarred scalp were touching. I learned my lesson, I was taking the pain meds at the water fountain on my way home from the surgery. I had 5 procedures and probably should have had one more, but I had enough plastic surgery and decided to leave it alone.

September 1978, Mr. St. Mary's College, Freshman year

After a non-eventful but relaxing summer, it was time to go to college. What had seemed like a long shot just one year before was now a reality. My mother, dad and sisters helped my brother and me pack up and move into our dorm rooms at the Mount. Tom was starting his senior year. My room was on the first floor of Sheridan Hall room 108, my roommate, Mike Behrens was from Havertown, PA. We got everything moved into my dorm room and then we all went over to my brother's room. We said our goodbyes and my sisters said there were a couple of things they forgot to put in my room. What they put in my room behind my back was at least 10 stuffed animal ducks. These were given to me while I was recovering in the hospital. Why ducks? Well that was a nickname I was given in grade school and carried on by a few of my grade school/St.E's friends that had attended Prep.

Many people have asked me how I got the nickname and either I wouldn't tell them, or I would tell them I forgot. The real reason I didn't tell them is that the story was dumb. So here it is. At recess and afterschool 6 or 7 of us played basketball almost every day on a court behind the school. It was 1973-74 and the Boston Celtics were a very popular and successful team at the time. I've never liked the Celtics but that's beside the point. One of my friends named each one of us after a player on the team. One guy would be Dave Cowens, another was the great John Havlicek and so on. I was named after Donald "Duck" Chaney and the nickname stuck. That's the nickname story many people have asked about over the years and that dumb reason is why I never told it.

I was thinking that I would leave the nickname behind, but when my new roommate and his friends walked into our dorm room and saw my bed covered in stuffed animal ducks, I knew I was keeping that nickname.

Because of my injury, I was given a room on the first floor so that I wouldn't have to go up and down stairs. The bad part was it was the farthest dorm from the main school building and dining hall. It was probably a good thing in the long run as it forced me to walk long distances every day which built up my endurance. It had been 14 months since my injury, and I had developed a gait with a limp. I still dragged my right foot when I got tired and if I caught my toe on any raised pavement I would trip and fall hard to the ground. I usually ended up with scrapes and scars on my elbows, hands and knees. But falling in most scenarios where people saw me was more embarrassing to me than getting the scrapes. The other problem was I couldn't get up off the ground by myself. If people were around, they would help me up but if I fell and no one was around I would have to crawl to a chair or table or something that I could pull myself up on. I did not have strong balance. If someone accidentally pushed me, I would most likely fall.

I have fallen hundreds of times. I've fallen walking into job interviews, on dates, once on a people mover in a Phoenix airport, down stairs, upstairs, in a classroom, at business conferences and it is always very embarrassing. I'm not trying to get sympathy here I'm just trying to demonstrate that although most things were getting better, I was frequently reminded that I would always have to deal with the side effects of my injury. What people saw on the outside was my limp, but I also had some other issues that weren't as visible. I had chronically low blood pressure as a side effect of the spinal cord injury and the damage to my autonomic nervous system. I would sometimes get light headed getting out of bed in the morning or if I stood up too fast. I still had some loss of feeling in my legs and had a difficult time with the sense of hot and cold. If I wasn't careful, I could burn myself if water was too hot and the dexterity of the fingers on my right hand was still not very good. I had some spasticity that caused my muscles (mostly in my legs) to be tight and stiff on cold days.

Although I beat the odds of not needing to use a catheter to urinate, my bladder function was far from normal. When I had the urge to "go", I would have to find a bathroom quickly and then have the added stress of not being able to walk fast and worrying about tripping. I learned to plan and locate the closest bathroom when I arrived at my destination. Another issue was that my bladder issues caused me to have frequent bladder infections my first year after my injury. This included my entire freshman year in college. Some people close to me knew this but mostly I tried to keep it private. I was taking antibiotics for the chronic infection for months but like the other physical issues I had, the infection mysteriously went away after about a year and I've never had a problem since then. Just like the bleeding ulcer, my body had eventually healed itself and I guess you could also include walking again.

I'm still close friends with many of the people I met my freshman year. Of course, my longtime friend Shawn was also at school with me. I also met Bill

Young at my brother's party on the first weekend at school. Bill, who I call "Chairman", would be my roommate at the Mount for 3 years. We have been very close friends for almost 40 years. We were in each other's weddings. Both he and Shawn have been there in my most difficult times as well as some of my most enjoyable times. My other close Mount friends were Jerry "Sgrigs" Sgrignoli, Tom Looney and his roommate Pete Monahan.

I had a tough time academically my first semester and ended up on academic probation. I think I was overconfident coming from Georgetown Prep and the tough academic curriculum. I had what I'll call a "pep talk" from my parents, and I did better my second semester. It was a big adjustment from high school and being on my own for the first time. It was a real bonus having my brother there my first year. As a senior he knew all the angles including which classes to take and which teachers to stay away from. I got to know some of his friends and of course his roommate Joe Avallone. Tom played on the baseball team and I was an assistant to the team manager. The highlight being a spring break road trip to Florida for daily baseball games and all-night parties on Daytona Beach. When Tom's class graduated it was sad because not only was Tom leaving, so were some of his classmates I had become friends with. At the time,

Mt. St. Mary's was a small school of approximately 1600 students, (now 2,200) 400 in each class, so you get to know most people on campus. Most students lived on campus and being located in the small town of Emmitsburg, there wasn't much to do in town, so you got to know many students in all classes. I finished up freshman year and was looking forward to summer vacation.

In the summer my dad got me a job working as a cook at a Sears employee cafeteria in Washington DC. I liked to cook and had learned enough from my parents over the years to get by. I worked from 8am to 2pm and Tom came to work lunch with me and then he stayed until 6pm closing. I worked for a local restaurant legend, Philip "Maggie" Manganello. Maggie was a blast to work for and it seemed like he knew everyone in the city. He owned the famous Maggie's Pizza and Goal Post restaurants. He was close friends with many legendary Redskins football players, including quarterback Sonny Jurgensen. Maggie asked me if I would like to have lunch with Sonny and of course I wanted to meet one of my sports idols. The three of us had lunch at a nearby restaurant and although I was a little "under the weather" from being out the night before, I thoroughly enjoyed listening to them tell compromising stories of past and current players. Sonny telling stories of games he played in and the 1969 season under the legendary coach Vince Lombardi. While I was recovering in the hospital, Sonny was nice enough to autograph a picture to me that said, "Paul you'll soon be running for those touchdowns- Sonny."

September 1979, Sophomore year

I started my second year at the Mount residing in my brother's former dorm room in Pangborn Hall. His room, my room now, was on the first floor and was directly across from the stairwell that led to the 2nd and 3rd floors; the girls' floors. As sophomores we had some choice of where we wanted to live and some of my friends got rooms on my floor, including Shawn and Chairman.

I was hoping I would have a better year academically and so were my parents. I was a business and finance major, taking required accounting and economic courses as well as other courses required to earn a degree at a liberal arts college. In the fall, the Mount basketball season began, and I took over the public address announcers' job that was previously held by my brother. Before the season started, I walked over to the gym and found the head coach of the men's basketball team, Jim Phelan. I asked him if I could be the public address announcer for the basketball games and without hesitation he said yes. I was sure he knew I was Tom's brother. The job paid me a whopping $3 a game and for the next three years would give me a front row seat to some of the most exciting basketball games played.

"Voice" of the Mount

While on Christmas break Shawn and I took a trip to the Rusk Rehabilitation Center in Manhattan, NY. Doctors working at the Center, were interested in meeting me, hearing about my injury and rehab. So, my friend and copilot Shawn and I drove up to NYC for two days and I met many doctors and physical therapists. I was examined and I answered many questions. On that trip I was searching for answers to questions I had about my future physical prognosis. I spent many years looking for answers. Looking for anyone who had a similar injury as mine and recovered. I wanted to know what physical issues I might encounter as I got older. But I never got any answers. I would have to figure it out along the way.

Sophomore Year - Second Semester

Besides working as the PA announcer for the men's and women's basketball games, I also had a job working as a bartender at the on-campus bar called the Rathskeller or as we called it, the "Rat". Being in such a small town and having most students on campus, the Rat was a very popular place in the evenings and especially on the weekends. When we were in college the drinking age was 18. No matter where you were on campus during the early evening you usually took a late evening trip to the Rat to get some food and beers and see what was happening before heading back to your dorm room.

After returning from spring break in March of 1980, we were told that a close friend of ours, Jay Scully, had died over the break after suffering a head injury. Jay was from Montclair, New Jersey and lived in the room next to me. Jay and I spent a lot of time together watching sports and listening to music and he was an Oklahoma Sooners fan just like me. He was an incredible lacrosse player, a lover of reggae music, smooth jazz, big band music and was a friend to us all. For me that was the first time I had lost a close friend. We all went to Jay's funeral and grew up a few years more that day.

Jay and me at a M*A*S*H party

September 1980, Junior year

It didn't take more than a year to realize how good my college experience had been. Two years had flown by with two years left. We were the upperclassmen now. We thought we had it all figured out. I had a core group of friends including Shawn, Jerry Sgrignoli, Tom Castaldi, Tom Looney, Pete Monahan and joining me and the Chairman were roommates Mark Hutton, Jerry O'Hara and Chris Delmonte. We took up residence in a three-bedroom apartment on the first floor; the soon to be very popular C-22. The newly built apartment buildings were only a year old and were luxurious compared to the older dorm rooms on campus. We decided to build a large bar at one end of our family room with a built-in stereo system and refrigerator. C-22 became a hot spot for late night parties after the Rat closed. I tried to balance the academics that college provides with the social aspects and looking back, I now realize I wasted a lot of learning opportunities. That year I took more classes focusing on my business major and I started to improve my grades.

C-22 "Bar" (What's with the pineapple?)

In the fall, the Mount basketball team got off to a fast start and by the end of the season the team was 28-3 and heading to the NCAA Division II tournament. After three epic wins at home in Memorial Gymnasium, the team headed to Springfield, Massachusetts for the Final Four. The school-chartered buses which were loaded with hundreds of students and twice as many coolers. We took over a hotel and got the party going early Friday. We must have accounted for almost a quarter of the crowd and with that semi-home court advantage, we won Friday night's game and would play for the division II national championship Saturday night. The bathtubs were filled with beer and the champagne was on ice when we left for the game. I, like many of the students, had our faces painted blue and white but the unbelievable season did not have the storybook ending. We lost a very close game to a team from Florida. That didn't stop the celebration as we partied well into the early hours. Many players came to our hotel and celebrated with us. I don't need to describe the quietest bus ride back to campus on Sunday. One of the last people on our bus was the Chairman. He stepped on board the quiet bus, looked at the bus driver and said, "take me to an aspirin factory."

September 1981, Senior year

Billy, Chris and I moved into a two-bedroom unit directly across from our junior year apartment, with Jerry and Mark living next door. We could have all stayed in C-22, but there was too much damage to our apartment and none of us could handle that much partying again. Besides, they made us take the bar down before we went home for the Summer. Senior year was very enjoyable. We were the big shots on campus. All of us were handling our academic courses to make sure we would graduate in the Spring. I continued to work at the Rat and announce the basketball games.

My sister Marian decided to follow Tom and me and attend the Mount and then Diane would enroll a year later. As a freshman, Marian had her own group of friends, and I would often spot her at some of our parties just like I had done my freshman year with Tom. I was completing the necessary courses for my business and finance degree and taking some other courses like astronomy and theater to complete the 120 credits I needed to graduate.

In the Spring of my senior year, I got the chance to drive across the country in a Winnebago with 8 other classmates. We left on Friday April 2, after our classes ended and returned 2 weeks later, on the 16th. Shawn, Jerry and I celebrated our birthdays during the trip. We drove from Emmitsburg, MD to San Diego, CA in a little over 2 days each of us taking a turn driving. We made trips to the San Diego Zoo, saw Diana Ross in concert and a day/night trip to Los Angeles. During the day we went to Universal Studios and in the evening, while on Sunset Boulevard, we were pulled over by the LAPD. All we were doing was asking a couple of well-dressed ladies on the street for directions. The cops didn't buy it and told us to head on back home to San Diego. On the way back home to Maryland we made stops at the Hoover Dam, the Grand Canyon, and Las Vegas. I think it was the first time any of us had been there. Some gambled and some did some sightseeing. After about 10 hours of fun we got back in our motorhome tired and almost broke and we made our way back home. When we made it back to school, we were dirty, exhausted but very happy to be back in one piece. We were welcomed home as semi celebrities.

Getting Ready to head to San Diego

We all finished the year completing our classes and attending some senior parties. We each had a fantastic college experience and all that was left was graduation and on with the rest of our lives. Those four years left an indelible mark on me. I am still very close to my core friends and when we get together, which is more frequently now, we retell many of our Mount experiences although the stories may be embellished a little bit more now. We graduated on May 28, 1982 after spending a week in Ocean City. We had left it all on the field.

I didn't have any job prospects lined up after graduation and I wasn't thinking about job prospects at all anyway. What I needed was a rest. In the Summer of 1982, I went back to work at the Sears cafeteria with Maggie and Tom. In July, Shawn and I organized the annual summer party at a hotel in Silver Spring, Md. It was a great success as many of our college friends came into town for the event.

One thing that had been bothering me for many years was my right knee. I had chronic pain in my knee and was getting cortisone shots for a couple of years to help with the pain. What started as a football injury in grade school had most likely been exacerbated by the way I walked. In September 1982, I underwent arthroscopic surgery on my knee to repair ligament and cartilage damage. While I was recovering from surgery, my sister Christine got me a part time job at the Mortgage company where she was working in Arlington Virginia. That part time job soon turned into a full-time job and started my 25 years in the mortgage banking industry.

I spent the next 3 years working for different single-family mortgage lenders. In 1983 I left home and rented a townhouse in Kensington, Maryland with Shawn and another Mount friend. I started dating a girl I knew from college, Mary Schantz and we were married in Rochester, NY in August 1985. We lived in

Kensington, MD before buying a townhouse in Burtonsville, MD, and then finally moving to Vienna, VA. in 1991. In 1986, I got a job working in the loan servicing department of a multifamily lender in Georgetown. Our company would lend money for apartment buildings and my department would collect payments, pay taxes & insurance and make sure the buildings were keeping up with necessary repairs. I didn't spend too long at one job. I was recruited by other multifamily lenders to take a better job and a significant salary increase.

Also, in the mid-eighties, some of the Maryland area Mount baseball players and some of our local friends formed a softball team. I was the coach. The team was sponsored by a local bar, Manny's, and for many years we were pretty good. The best part of playing softball is the socializing after the games. Most of the core of the team, which included my brother, played together for over 15 years. On one particular post-game celebration at Manny's, a few of us, including Shawn, were drinking shots, many shots, along with our beers. The empty tower of shot glasses fell over when the table got bumped. The glasses broke, and one hit my knee cap. A large deep gash opened, and the blood was flowing. A barely sober friend drove Shawn and me to Suburban hospital ER. To say I was drunk was an understatement and I was getting drunker from the shots we just drank. The shot glass had cut my knee down to the bone. It took a lot of stitches to close it. I'm sure they used lidocaine, but it didn't really matter. I couldn't feel anything in my condition. I was there for a couple of hours and was sobering up when a few of the emergency room staff stopped by and said they remembered me when I was brought in after my diving accident. They were very happy to see I was doing so well. I thanked them for helping me that night. I can remember getting home and telling that story to my wife. She wasn't amused.

For many years after my accident, I got a few calls from people who had heard of my accident and recovery. Either they had a family member who had a similar accident or had a friend who had been injured. They asked me if I would visit them in the hospital. I probably made at least 15 visits over a 25-year period. At first, I was hesitant and nervous. I didn't know what to say but after a few visits I got more comfortable. I would answer their questions and give them encouragement. Coming from someone who had been in their place carried more weight. I spent time with the parents telling them to stay positive and the course of action my parents had taken with my rehab. I would leave them my phone number if they wanted to talk. Some called most didn't. I did receive a few nice letters thanking me for visiting their child. That meant a lot to me. I still have those letters. I really enjoyed those visits, but I learned to tone down their expectations because my case was the exception not the rule.

In 1988, I left the commercial mortgage world and started a small computer company on the Maryland eastern shore (Stevensville) called Micro Support. By small I mean me and another guy I had worked with at a previous mortgage company. We were developing software and selling desktop PC's that were getting extremely popular at the time. My brother Tom came on to help us a few months after we got things started. The company closed just shy of one year. Although the paychecks were sporadic, I learned a great deal about computer hardware and software, and I learned how hard it is to start and run a business. The biggest thing was just how much capital it takes. My brother and I drove back and forth over the bay bridge every day and I considered it an enjoyable learning experience. I had also found something I really liked - computer technology.

After we closed Micro Support, I went back to work in the computer department of a commercial mortgage company in 1989. The bank hired me to help them with their mortgage systems and assist in their loan servicing department. At that time, there weren't PC's on each employee's desk like there is today. Most mortgage banking software was developed for mainframe computers. Some companies placed one PC in each department for writing letters. As that company was slowly going out of business, I left and joined the Washington Mortgage Group in 1990. WMG was the commercial lender for the National Bank of Washington. NBW at the time was one of the oldest banks in Washington DC. I was hired to be the Multifamily loan servicing manager. On my first day I met Carole Kennedy. Carole was the single-family loan servicing manager. At the time Mary and I were living in Burtonsville Maryland. It was a long traffic filled commute, but the job and the company seemed the right fit for me. It seemed I was working for a company that had a lot of potential.

Carole and me at an office Christmas party

In May 1991, my niece Katherine (Katy) was born. Tom and Suzy asked me to be Katy's Godfather and of course I accepted the honor. Katy is a beautiful, funny, successful woman and it's great that she lives close by and visits often. The other significant addition to my household was a kitten that I named Zinger. Mary's brother thought we needed a pet and showed up for a visit with a gift for us.

For the next couple of years that I worked at Washington Mortgage, I worked my way up the corporate ladder to Vice President in charge of loan servicing and Carole was promoted to AVP. We made a formidable team. The company grew by purchasing smaller companies around the country. I began to travel a few times a month to visit banks and attend conferences and like many business meetings, there's work and play. The stereotype that a lot of relationships are developed on golf courses are very true. The travel to many cities, San Francisco and New Orleans were two of my favorites, was initially exciting, but after a couple of years of it, the traveling got old very fast. It became necessary to keep my golf clubs in the trunk of my car because if you are part of a fast-growing financial company many individuals and businesses want to be involved with you, so they offer to wine and dine you. When my boss Howard couldn't attend or travel to these events, he sent me or Carole. Golf outings, expensive dinners and tickets to sporting events or concerts. I was working hard and having the time of my life.

Prior to an important business meeting

In May of 1994, Katy's brother Thomas was born. Currently Thomas, who was an All-American lacrosse player at LSU, has started to work in commercial real estate in Washington, DC.

Everything seemed to be going well. Well, not everything. My wife and I were having trouble in our marriage. In 1995, after 10 years of marriage, Mary and I divorced. We had what I thought was a good marriage, but Mary wanted something different in her life at the time. We separated for a year and went through marriage counseling. Mary had gotten her own apartment while we tried to make things work and even moved back into our home for a couple of months. But in the end, it was best for us to go our separate ways. Mary moved to New York City and I stayed in our house in Vienna with Zinger. Other than my divorce in 1995, the 90's were probably the most successful and fun years of my life.

In May of 1997, my second niece Megan was born. Obviously, we were all happy, but my mother and dad were very excited for their third grandchild. Megan is pretty and smart and currently a senior at Auburn University. Time sure flies.

Katy, Thomas and Megan

It was also around this time that I met Carole's best friend Carrie who was visiting from South Dakota. Carrie is a wonderful person, a Navy veteran and has been a surgical nurse for over 25 years. We seemed to meet at the right times in our lives. We dated for a few years, going to the beach on weekends and taking trips around the country. Happily, the bonus of our relationship was getting to know her daughter, Christina. Although we are no longer dating, we remain close friends today, even though she's a Steeler fan.

Christina & Carrie

Golfing Highlights

As I have said, I grew up a sports junkie. I loved and played just about every sport with a ball. Basketball was probably my favorite sport, but I also played golf whenever I could growing up, and in high school. After my injury, the only sport activity I could continue to play was golf. Golf is a great activity that can be played your whole life if you can physically swing a club. You don't have to be good, just understand the rules and the etiquette and you'll have a great day. I've mentioned my business "meetings" on the course, but I want to relate one funny golf story. I was attending a mortgage banking conference in San Francisco. On Saturday before the conference started, the Mortgage Bankers Association held a golf tournament. A handful of my fellow work friends played, and I got into a foursome with my friend, Scott, who worked in our Los Angeles office. As the day was ending, one of the last holes we played was a closest to the pin contest. A company had sponsored the hole and had set up cameras and had announcers on the hole like a televised professional tournament.

Here's the important part of the story. We had a few beers during the day, and as we got to the last few holes our playing partner pulled out a joint. I didn't want to be unsociable, so I smoked a little and passed it to the rest of the players. Of course, we knew nothing about the closest to the pin hole coming up next. I stumbled out of the cart on #17 and a guy was telling us about the contest. The hole was a 147-yard, par 3. I couldn't hit the ball as far as I did before I got hurt. I had to use a lower iron to get any distance. I really enjoy playing and I scored between 95-105. But at our level it's more about the experience. I pulled out a 5 iron, teed the ball up and realized that I was a little woozy. I addressed the ball and swung as hard as I could, and I made the best swing of the day. The ball headed right for the pin. I knew it was on the green, but I couldn't see how close to the hole it was. Everyone at the tee was cheering. The announcer asked me what club I used, and I told him a 9 iron. Scott heard me and then he changed his club to a sand wedge not wanting to hit over the green. But his ball landed 20 yards short of the green. I was waiting for him in the cart and he asked how I hit a 9 iron that far and I confessed I'd used a 5 iron. We both laughed all the way to the green. When I got to the green, I could see that my ball was 4 feet from the hole. Amazing! I made the tricky downhill putt for a birdie and it turned out that I was second closest to the pin. I probably hadn't had a birdie in 10 years. I won a Big Bertha driver at the awards dinner. Quite a story and quite a day.

Another highlight in the 90's was getting an opportunity from a coworker at WMF to play a round of golf with Hubert Green. Hubert Green won 26 professional golf tournaments, including two major championships: the 1977 U.S. Open and the 1985 PGA Championship. He was inducted into the World Golf Hall of Fame in 2007. I flew down to his home club near Pensacola, Florida and played 18 holes of golf with him and 2 other work associates. He asked me to ride in his cart with him for a few holes and during the round he gave us a few pointers. After 9 holes I was more relaxed and enjoyed the round. He told us not to take pictures during the round because he would take as many with him when we finished. Watching someone that talented up close gave me a different level of respect for just how good professional athletes are.

Me with Hubbie Green and WMF coworkers

Beulah Beach Club

In the Spring of 1997, I decided to build a pool in my backyard. I had thought about it for a couple of years and after my divorce I needed to change things up a little. My house became very popular on the summer weekends. It was nice to have friends and family come to swim and cookout. A lot of my friend's kids learned how to swim there, and I hosted Katy, Thomas and Megan's birthday and graduation parties. We had my parents 50th wedding anniversary celebration and Shawn and Lisa's wedding rehearsal dinner there too. We always remember that rehearsal dinner party because we all watched O J Simpson ride around Los Angeles in the white Bronco. Of course, it was the perfect venue to host my annual summer bash. At some point I started calling my home, on Beulah Rd., The Beulah Beach Club. Every summer in early July, I had my summer party and there were some epic bashes. I had a Beulah Beach Club logo designed and had tee shirts and drink koozies made. I gave out the shirts at the parties. I had a lot of help from family and friends planning, setting up, grilling and Sunday clean up - a total group effort.

Beulah Beach Club Logo

Over the 20 years I hosted the party, the crowd was anywhere between 25 and 50 friends and family. It was a good way for all of us to stay in touch. Highlights of the party were floating firework displays, a potato gun (Google it), and the famous ice luge. Of course, getting a seat in the hot tub in the late evening was the place to be. Many things have happened in my life over the last 25 years, but the one constant has been my home. The business traveling, the long hours at the office, and vacation trips, yet as we all know there's no place like home and pulling into the driveway makes my problems, big or small, just a little easier to deal with.

Summer party with cousin Cathy, my mother, Uncle Jules (my Godfather) and my dad

Cousins Mike & Jim (Ice Luge) with Marian

Beulah Beach

I worked at Washington Mortgage for close to 8 years. I worked my way up to Group Vice President in charge of the Loan Servicing and Information Technology departments. I traveled all over the country to attend conferences, evaluate potential companies and meet with our bankers. As the company grew, Carole, now a VP, took over the Loan Servicing department and I was the head of the IT department. In mid-1997, the company went public and the culture of the company changed drastically. Washington Mortgage had gone from a very successful privately owned "family" type company to a cold corporate culture run by a faceless board of directors.

I'm obviously still bitter after all these years. I kept my title but was moved into another position. The board was replacing many managers with people with Ivy League MBAs. The decision to go public couldn't have been done at a worse time. A couple months later the real estate market took a downturn and the company was sold to a large insurance company to avoid bankruptcy. One of the last business trips I took at WMF was an annual multifamily conference that in January of 1998 was held in San Francisco. Although the real estate market was hit hard in October, that January WMF as well as many commercial mortgage companies were riding high. Our company sent close to 100 employees from all over the country. I took vacation days and went out a few days early with Carrie. Carole joined us, and we spent a couple of days sightseeing in San Francisco. On Saturday morning we went to the Pebble Beach Pro-Am golf tournament and spent the afternoon in Carmel. On Sunday the conference started but we had a memorable weekend for sure. I had scheduled a tee time at Pebble Beach for Tuesday with some of our customers, but a massive rain storm closed the course and my one and only chance to play the iconic golf course was lost. I was at a peak in my life and sometimes there is only one way you can go when you're riding that high.

The commercial real estate market took a swift downturn in October 1998, and I was caught up in a massive employee layoff. It was personally devastating. I was one of the initial members that started the company. I had worked my way up and had given my best to make the company successful. It felt like a family. But I would learn a painful but valuable lesson. Business is business and not to get personally involved. Once the company had gone public all bets were off. It's not about the employees it's about the bottom line. To make matters worse, I held onto my shares of stock as it went from $33 to $9. Our president told us that it was a bad sign for executives to sell stock. By the time I left my shares were worthless.

In November of 1998, right after I was let go at Washington Mortgage, I took a job at a small multifamily company in Bethesda, Maryland as the head of the Asset Management department. The commercial mortgage business is a close industry in and around the D.C. Metro area. I had a good reputation and had worked with many people over the last 15 years. Friends and coworkers move from company to company. When you need a job, you contact your friends that you worked with before. It was a small privately held company and I had worked previously with many of the employees including my boss Howard and my friend Doug Nadeau from WMF.

It was about this time that I started to notice that I would lose my balance sometimes while I was walking. I can recall walking close to the walls down hallways. I would stumble and need to touch the wall to keep my balance. Most days this wasn't an issue but every now and then it would happen. I tripped and fell a few times. I didn't have any type of exercise plan, so I thought maybe that was the problem. In my mind I figured that at some point later in life my diving injury would become a problem physically, but I didn't think it would happen at age 39. I had lower back pain which was exacerbated by the way I walked. I have had right knee pain for many years which I attribute to my gait and the limping and it sometimes causes right hip pain. But I have learned to live with these issues. They are my normal. I take Aleve and Advil and have a prescription for pain medication which I take when the pain gets extreme. The pain can get bad if I'm on my feet for a long time or if I play a round of golf. But I've never liked taking pain meds, thank goodness, so the pain must be pretty extreme. I use ice packs a lot, which really works as well as anything some days. I've had spinal nerve blocks, but they have had little effect. Having to deal with various levels of pain for such a long period of time, my tolerance has grown over the years. It is a rarity when I don't have some body part nagging me. The end of the day is worse, but I don't let it overcome me. When I'm working on something, driving somewhere I'm distracted from it and the more I move the less pain I feel.

Back to the job situation: After two years of dealing with a boss, the accounting manager, who didn't have a clue about technology or asset management. I was at a time in my life and career when I wouldn't put up with ineptness. When I was younger, I would just go along with my boss when I knew he was wrong. But not now. I butted heads with him and became a thorn in his side which eventually got me fired. The company and I came to an agreement. They would pay my contract and I would leave quietly. I did. I put my check in the bank and spent a few weeks poolside at Beulah Beach. The only good thing that came out of working there was meeting two good friends of mine Mark Bultman and Jeff Erhardt. Mark and his wife Carla now live in Chicago with their three boys but luckily Jeff lives close to me in Vienna with his wife Sheila and their daughters Emma and Grace.

I wanted to do something other than commercial banking and I had been getting more involved with computers, so I enrolled in a school to get my network engineering and data communications degree. I really enjoyed being back in the classroom. I focused on the work, studied hard and finished first in the class. If I only would have tried half as hard in college but I didn't know any better at the time. In April of 2000, I got my network engineering degree. Now what?

After graduating, I worked part time as a network administrator after I got out of school until the fall of 2000 and then I couldn't find any other technology jobs. I didn't have the experience necessary for the jobs and salary I wanted. The job search continued through most of 2001. I somewhat enjoyed being unemployed except for the part where you have a mortgage and car payments and bills to pay. I was using a home equity loan and withdrawing money from my IRA. I was working out more and that was helping my physical conditioning but the stress of not working for this long was getting to me. I was interviewing here and there through the summer. I had some job offers but the salary was too low. My experience was in Mortgage banking. I got a call from a friend who I worked with at Washington Mortgage telling me about an opportunity at Reilly Mortgage. Reilly Mortgage was a competitor of WMF, and I knew many of their employees. Some of them had worked with Carole and me at WMF when I was the Loan Servicing manager. I had been asked to come in for an interview the second week in September for a position in the Information Technology department. The position was assistant IT manager in charge of implementing a mortgage origination software package that I had implemented at WMF. The interview was postponed because of 9/11. Because of the state of the country after the terrible attack, I didn't think they would be hiring for a long time. But I finally interviewed for the position and got the job. I started in October 2001. I was extremely happy to be working again. It was a good job in a successful company, and it was close to home.

In June of 2002, I got a call from my sister-in-law Suzy, who was at Megan's preschool and saw a sign posted saying that a 6-month-old black Labrador Retriever needed to be adopted and according to Suzy, he needed to be adopted soon, if you know what I mean. I was living alone, and my roommate Zinger had died a couple of years earlier, so I agreed to adopt him, if I would get some family help when I traveled. So, a few days later, my mother, Suzy, Megan and I went to see Boomer who was living at a Veterinary office in Rockville. At the time his name was Lejeune. I knew once I saw him, he would be coming home and a few days later he came home to Beulah Beach. When he jumped into the pool and started to swim around my father said "Boomer, you hit the lottery." The truth was we all had.

Boomer

In my time at Reilly Mortgage, I was exposed to many cutting-edge software programs. Because of my mortgage finance experience and my computer knowledge I became a liaison between each department and the IT department. I was able to understand the users' needs and then help design the programs that would make their jobs easier. I enjoyed the job; the pay was good, and it was close to home. My friend Tony Martin, a consultant to the IT department, was nice enough to teach me a little computer programming. We were writing programs for the Human Resources, Accounting, and Asset Management departments. I was learning the basics as we were developing an Asset Management program for the company. But we all know nothing good lasts forever. At least that's my experience. In July of 2005, in preparation for the sale of the company, many employees including myself were let go to cut costs. I had been told I was safe by my manager but as "cut" day got closer I had a feeling he was lying to me. The day of the layoffs I was walking so poorly that I used a cane, actually a shillelagh, I had bought in Ireland. It was the first time I had used a cane at work. I had no personal items in my office at Reilly. The last job I left I was carrying out pictures and miscellaneous personal items. That wouldn't happen again. One thing I learned in the many companies I worked for is it's a business first and foremost. You get sent to team building seminars and are told by executives that we are like a family. But as soon as things go bad in the business people get laid off and told it's nothing personal. The two jobs I got laid off from, I was promoted months earlier. When I worked at Reilly, I never looked at it as any more than a job. I worked very hard there but always realized that I could be let go or find something better at any time. My last business trip that I would take was a trip to Las Vegas for a programming conference in June with Tony. Like I've said before about these "business" trips they're a little work and a little play. A couple of weeks after I got back from the trip, I did get "the call" from HR. I dropped off my key and they asked me if I needed any help with my stuff and I said I didn't have anything there. It was an easier exit but most likely my last.

I had a feeling for a couple of years prior to my layoff, that this would probably be my last job where I would be able to commute to an office and work 40 or more hours a week. My physical condition was making it harder to get through each day. My balance issues were continuing to very slowly get worse and my pain at the end of the work days was getting bad. Real bad. My lower back and knees were the biggest problems. I treated it with ice and pain meds. I was getting as much physical therapy as my insurance would cover - 12 visits a year. That would help for a while, but I knew I had to find a long-term solution.

May 2003, Ireland

On the brighter side, my sister Christine and I took a 10-day trip to Ireland in 2003. We flew into Shannon on the west coast of the country, rented a car and drove, on the wrong side of the road, to Dublin on the east coast. We stopped in bed and breakfast homes along the way and 2 nights in very luxurious hotels. We took the southern route and made stops in Kilkenny, Kenmare, Cobh, Waterford, Cork. We spent two days in the coastal town of Kinsale, which reminded me of Annapolis; and of course, we visited the Blarney Stone and spent three days in Dublin before flying home. We had a great trip seeing restored as well as run down castles. We followed our own agenda and navigated narrow and winding "roads" taking turns driving on the wrong side of the road. I was able to get around the country well enough to see most everything on our agenda. I'm so glad we went.

So far in this book, I've tried to recount my life 28 years post injury. My early childhood, my high school and college years and my business career. The reason why I recounted my favorite stories is to tell you how fortunate I was to have had such a wonderful time, traveling in the US and in Europe visiting beautiful cities, spending time with old friends and meeting new ones. I was 45 years old and the average life expectancy for someone with my level of spinal cord injury is approximately 40 years. (fscip.org). I was aware how very lucky I was to have gotten a second chance after suffering such a terrible accident. I didn't take it for granted.

My thoughts during these years was that if my physical status stayed close to the same as it had been over these years, that I could hopefully get to age 60 or 65. That's what I was hoping for in my 30's and 40's. I thought I would start to have some significant physical problems after that. That was my plan. But as I've said, I was noticing some changes in the early 2000s and I knew I would have to find a way to address these new problems or learn to adapt to these challenges.

In August of 2005, I was given my exit pay and 3 months of paid health insurance, and before my insurance expired, I went for a physical. I had been getting physicals annually for many years. I consider myself a healthy person, low blood pressure, low cholesterol, an occasional cold but no serious health issues. Well, just a broken neck and paralysis but who's counting. My main concern was my lower back, knee pain and the continuing balance issues that started a couple of years prior. For the severe knee and back pain, I would use Advil, Aleve and Vicodin. A 60 pill Vicodin prescription would last me most of the year. When the pain got too much to handle, I would take half of 1 pill, usually at the end of the day, and that would get me through the pain. I had these pain killers available to me for many years. As I've said, I don't like taking prescription medication but occasionally I can get overwhelmed by my pain and they do help.

I went to my appointment in September of 2005. I have a GP, Dr. Huang, whom I have been seeing for over 5 years. I'm sure you have seen the forms you have to complete and the page with a long list of ailments that you check yes or no. For example, kidney disease Y or N, high blood pressure Y or N, and so on. When he had finished my physical exam, Dr. Huang saw on my form that I had checked yes for hepatitis. That question had been on every physical history form I had ever completed for over 25 years and I had never checked yes but for some reason, this time I did. I explained to him that in the hospital after my spinal cord injury, I had a bleeding ulcer and needed multiple pints of blood and developed some form of blood hepatitis in the hospital. At that time, it was called non-A or non-B hepatitis.

According to Wikipedia, in the US, blood, used for transfusions, was not screened for hepatitis until

1992. You've seen the ads on TV for Hep-C drug treatment and for people to get tested. An estimated 130-200 million people, mostly baby boomers, are infected with the disease. Many people don't know about their status because they don't have any symptoms and don't see any reason to be tested. It is believed that only 5–50% of those infected in the United States and Canada are aware of their status.

My doctor asked me if he could test my blood for the infection along with the other usual blood work. I agreed and as you might have guessed, I tested positive for Hepatitis C. I was shocked, but I wasn't sure how serious it was. So I had been infected for 28 years and had no symptoms. I had two choices: one, do nothing and continue to monitor the situation with annual blood tests, or two, get treatment now while I was younger and healthy and would be better equipped to withstand the side effects. The second option made sense to me at the time, but I wasn't prepared for the severe side effects of the medication that would hit me hard.

The treatment was very expensive. but Dr. Huang sent me to a company that had an opening in a two-year trial for their new hepatitis medications and had gotten good results - 50-60% "cure" rate. There is no cure for Hepatitis C. Medical professionals consider a cure to mean that Hep-C is not found in the blood six months after completing treatment.

To get accepted into the trial, I had to complete a long questionnaire about myself and my medical history. I had to agree to many tests and to follow the treatment guidelines. I had to have a liver biopsy, a painful procedure, to assess any liver damage. I decided to do it without anesthesia because the puncture is quick, and I hate anesthesia. Christine took me to the hospital where I spent most of the day either waiting for or recovering from a 30-minute procedure. The test showed no damage to or cirrhosis of my liver. It was as healthy as most 46-year-old livers should be. I had to take the medications as required and follow their trial protocols. The treatment in 2005 consisted of using pegylated interferon in combination with ribavirin. Unfortunately, these medications are very expensive and have significant side effects.

According to the website of the company that made the medication the Hematologic toxicities include anemia and leukopenia. These can be managed with close monitoring, use of growth factors, or dose reductions. Depression also can be caused or exacerbated by these medicines. Influenza-like symptoms of fatigue, nausea, and mild fevers can be helped by quality patient education and support including frequent office visits. Data from randomized controlled trials demonstrating improvements in long-term survival because of treatment are not yet available, but it appears that patients who have no detectable virus six months after treatment have a good chance of remaining virus free for at least five years.

I walked (without a cane) into my first appointment in November of 2005 and was given my medications for the first month. I was also shown how to use the pre-filled syringes to inject myself with the interferon once a week. I had never gotten used to injections even after the hundreds of shots and blood draws I had in the hospital. I always look in another direction and just the smell of the alcohol wipes starts some anxiety. I had no idea how I was going to inject myself once a week. But I somehow found a way and did the injections and took the pills and started the 11-month treatment period. The nausea and vomiting started about 3 weeks into the treatment usually the day after the shot. The hair loss started about 3 months in. The depression started about two months in and got bad in months 8-11. I knew it was one of the side effects of the medication, but I had some very dark days. The ironic part of the whole ordeal was I started the treatment healthy and feeling great but with every injection and pill I took, I got sicker. I would start to feel a little better and then it would be time for another shot. The treatment made me so tired that I couldn't do much outside the house. I wasn't working, and I wouldn't have been able to work if I had a job. Some days I would be driving somewhere and had to pull over to rest for 30 minutes. I would get home and had to sleep.

Halfway into my treatment, I needed to use a walker to attend my bi-monthly meetings with the trial staff. I would fill out questionnaires about my mental state. For instance, on a scale of 1-10 how likely are you having suicidal thoughts. My energy was so low because my red blood counts were low, so a few months into the treatment, I gave myself Procrit injections. The good news was that the Hep-C counts were improving. But I had to finish the 11-month trial period. In addition to needing a cane and sometimes a walker, I also had to purchase a lift chair recliner for my home. I was so weak that I couldn't get out of my recliner without help. What I thought was a temporary loss of physical strength lasted for many years and that chair was extremely helpful. If I could do it all over again, I wouldn't have gone through the trial.

An interesting thing happened in December of 2005 while I was in the middle of my treatment. A former coworker at Washington Mortgage asked me to help him with a government bid to purchase and service some low interest loans. I told him my current physical situation and that I wasn't sure I could work every day. I needed the money, so I gave it a try. I met him in his office in Arlington, Virginia. His office was in the same building, the same floor and the same office area where I had my first job out of college. The temporary job Christine had gotten me at Congressional Mortgage while I was recovering from knee surgery. What were the odds? The job lasted 6 weeks and I knew I couldn't work anymore. A couple of months earlier I had applied for permanent disability and now I knew I was going to need it. In February of 2006, I was approved for Social Security Disability Insurance (SSDI).

One of the challenges with writing this book in 2017 is trying to remember how I was doing physically during certain years and time periods. The best way I have found is to remember certain events or trips and then I can recall my physical condition at that time. For instance, the last trip I made while I was working at Reilly Mortgage was in June of 2005. It was an IT conference in Las Vegas. I was using a cane to get around the conference and the casino and I used a wheelchair in the airports. Because I was not working after July of 2005, my experiences in the years following are sometimes difficult to write about. I know I was in a slow physical decline and I spent a

lot of time at home.   The months and years can run
together.

Dad

In the Spring of 2006, my father who had been fighting esophageal cancer off and on for a few years stopped his chemo treatments and agreed to home hospice care. His cancer battle started with his diagnosis in 2003. I believe it started with difficulty swallowing which led to weight loss and then to his diagnosis of esophageal cancer. Who knows exactly what caused his cancer? Anyway, it doesn't matter how, he had it and he tried every treatment possible. One procedure he underwent was performed at the NIH. His tumor was removed as well as most of his esophagus. The stomach and remaining esophagus were then reattached. His surgery was successful and later he had radiation and chemotherapy. I remember that he couldn't eat very much, and he lost more weight, but these treatments bought him another year or so until the cancer came back. Suzy was very instrumental in getting him through the surgery and treatments. She researched and made calls and got him into NIH and got him to his doctor appointments. Along with dad's toughness, Suzy was a big reason we had dad around for a couple extra years. One of the big reasons that I overcame some of my challenges was my dad teaching me to be tough at a young age. When you were knocked down you got up. "Walk it off" he'd yell from the sideline and those last three years of his life he showed us all how to be tough. I can only imagine how bad he felt the last six months but when any of us visited him he hid it well. He always wanted us to stay and have lunch or dinner. He was the gracious host right to the end. I can remember him making sure his caregiver had something to drink or eat. He didn't want to be a bother. The last couple of weeks we had a bed set up in the dining room of our house, just like after I came home from the hospital. We would take turns visiting, making sure one of us was there most of the day. My mother at the same time had been diagnosed with early onset Alzheimer's disease. So, my dad's illness was especially difficult for her to deal with. All our family was close by, Marian had to make many trips from Delaware. Dad's friends and relatives visited. My dad was a well-loved person. On the Sunday before he died, he wanted all of us over to the house. After dinner he gave a well thought out gift to each of his grandchildren. He gave his car to Katy who would be driving in a couple of years, he gave Megan a new laptop for school and he gave Thomas a small row boat to go fishing and crabbing. It was something my dad did growing up in the summers he spent in Bay

Ridge on the Chesapeake Bay. Today, Thomas keeps his boat at Christine's house in Easton, Maryland. The next week Dad's condition was getting worse and on Sunday, May 7th, Dad passed away in his sleep early in the evening with all his family around him.

His funeral was a few days later with a big party after the service at my brother's house. It was the kind of celebration he would have loved. Family, friends and relatives and many people that got to know him over the years. Too bad that we can't attend the one party that brings everyone that loves us together. It doesn't make sense. My dad was cremated and a month later was interred in the Arlington National Cemetery's columbarium following an emotional service, complete with a 21-gun salute. My dad had struggled over the last 3 years but rarely showed it. He taught me many things. He was kind and funny and generous and tough right to the end. It's been over 12 years since he died, and I miss him, but I can still hear his encouraging words when I need them.

Mother and Dad

During the summer of 2006, I was using a wheelchair to go anywhere that required walking any significant distances, and because of not walking, my muscles were getting weaker. For that reason, my brother or one of my sisters had to drive me to my doctor or dentist appointments and wheel me into the office. The mental effects of the Hep-C treatment drugs were wearing me down. I got through it by focusing on one week at a time. Counting down the injections. I would finish the treatment in October and that was what I was focusing on. About 7 months into the treatment my weekly blood test showed no more signs of the hepatitis C virus. The treatment had worked so far. I would need to finish the program and be tested annually to make sure the virus was undetectable. In November of 2006 my sister Christine wheeled me into my final treatment appointment. One last blood draw and I went home. It was a couple of months before I started to feel better.

It was the start of 2007. I didn't have a job and I was on permanent disability. It was a good thing that my sister Diane was living with me. She helped me on bad days and there were many during my treatment. She made me meals, helped me with my laundry, and many other things I needed. I was spending a couple of mornings a week visiting my mother who was showing early signs of Alzheimer's disease. For the last couple of years, her short-term memory had been getting worse. She lived alone with her dog Jack and had to give up driving. All of us had a difficult time getting her to stop driving but eventually she did. She would not let us sell her car. She wanted it parked in her driveway and that was fine with us. I didn't realize until later how lucky I was to have spent so much more time with her because I wasn't working. I would bring her breakfast from McDonald's or we would have lunch. We would watch TV and do puzzles and talk. We reviewed her mail and her bills and made sure everything was taken care of.

She would meet me at the car, and we would walk arm in arm across the lawn and into the house. When it was time to leave, she would always walk me back to my car and thank me for visiting. I was using a cane at that time, but she provided me a wonderful person to lean on. All of us took turns helping my mother stay in her house. Laundry was done, groceries were bought, grass was cut, and everyone spent time with her. She would say "I haven't seen your brother in so long" and I would have to remind her that he had just been there yesterday. On the weekends we would try to get her and Jack to come over to visit me and Diane and Boomer. My mother was tough (as I've described) and wasn't going to hear any talk about moving her out of her home. Like a lot of families dealing with a similar situation, we were taking it a week at a time. The six of us got into a routine to help her and we did a good job. It is a tremendous strain on a family in a similar situation with only one or two caregivers.

As 2007 ended, my condition was about the same. I thought that I would have shaken off the effects of the Hep-C treatment, but I hadn't. I was spending more time at home and any thoughts of finding a job had gone out the window. When I went to the store or pharmacy, I had to find a nearby shopping cart to use to walk with. I was using a cane when I went out of the house. At home, my house was one level and not that big, so I could move from a piece of furniture to a wall to a table, kind of like a monkey swinging from vine to vine. I just couldn't admit to myself that I needed a cane full time. I thought if I started to rely on a cane, I would get used to it and of course there's the vanity thing. It wouldn't be too long before I started using two canes out of the house. My muscle spasticity was getting a little worse and my pain, although chronic, was manageable with NSAIDS and painkillers but it was wearing me down.

Transitions

Many of us have a parent or close relative who, due to an illness or just getting older, has had to transition from their long-time home to a smaller condo maybe to an assisted living facility. Some may continue to drive when they may be a danger to themselves or others on the road. Transitions like these are difficult for everyone. Nobody wants to admit they need help from someone or assistance from a medical device, a cane, walker or wheelchair. Sometimes our pride can get in the way. I know these transition situations very well as I've had more than a few transitions in my lifetime. I've done just about anything I could to avoid having to transition to the next thing.

My first transition was officially in 2007 but it should have been a year sooner. Following a year of hepatitis C treatment in 2006, I was physically and mentally exhausted. I started to lose my balance while walking sometimes, by tripping or stumbling and avoiding a fall by grabbing a wall or piece of furniture; other times by falling hard to the ground. I tripped and fell in a parking lot after a softball game and needed about 20 stitches above my eye. I should have been using a cane, but I didn't. I thought that I was still recovering from the treatment, but I was not getting better. I could get away without a cane around the house but not outside in wide open areas. So, instead of using a cane to get around, I would stay home missing out on many trips and other get-togethers with friends. Finally, in 2008, I started using a cane and then 2 canes later, but always later than I should have. I was lucky to avoid a serious injury.

Mother

In late April of 2008, my mother went to the hospital with extreme pain in her abdomen. She had been complaining off and on to us for a couple of weeks about it. We would ask her about it, and she would say she was fine. In her mental state, it was hard for us to know what was really going on with her physically. We had her visit her doctor once a month and she was on an Alzheimer's medication, which she may or may not have been taking. It was a downside to her living alone, but she was stubborn about her independence.

Her stomach pain got worse and in late April my Uncle JB took her to the hospital. They did some tests which showed that she had a substantial blockage in her intestines. They kept her in the hospital while they tried a procedure to untwist her intestines. We took turns staying with her, but the procedure didn't help. The doctor was trying anything he could other than surgery but eventually that was her only option. We all sat in the waiting room and a few hours into the surgery the doctor came out and told us that her intestines were very badly damaged and torn in some places and that she was suffering from an infection -

severe sepsis. The only thing he could do was stop the surgery and treat her with antibiotics. She was moved to intensive care. She was very sick. She seemed to understand the gravity of her situation and didn't want any further surgery. The hospital staff allowed her to stay in a nice private room where we could all visit. She watched the Kentucky derby with Christine on Saturday afternoon and was in good spirits almost rallying against her circumstances. On Sunday morning Diane and I went to visit her, and she was sleeping but her breathing wasn't good. It reminded me of the last day my father was alive. I called the rest of my family and my Uncle Chick, her brother, to come immediately. It wasn't more than a couple of hours later that my mother passed away in her sleep. It was two years after my father died on the Sunday after the Kentucky Derby, same as my dad. My mother hadn't suffered too long, and she stayed in her house until the end. We all knew she never would have accepted or even survived living in an assisted living or any other facility. It was a small consolation of her passing away. Her funeral was a week later, followed by a nice party, of course. Soon after she was placed in my father's vault at the columbarium at Arlington National Cemetery.

RICHARD J
BROWN
SSGT   USAF
1929   2006
HIS WIFE
JANE M
1929   2008

In June of 2008, I was having more pain in my hips. One morning I had a bad fall coming out of the bathroom. I got a pain spasm in my hip and my legs collapsed. I rolled my ankle injuring it badly. My entire foot was black and blue. I couldn't walk and needed in-home therapy. I had been going to therapy when I worked, but I hadn't been in a few years. I had also noticed that the left side of my body had been getting weaker. I never had any issues with my left side. For 30 years I had to compensate for my right leg and right hand being weak. Things were changing, and I couldn't figure out why. I had in-home therapy for 2 weeks and I was much better. I started using a walker. I needed to get back into a therapy program soon and stop my physical deterioration. The therapist I had used in the past recommended a PT named Valerie Gibson. She was the owner of a neurological therapy center close to me in Vienna called Advanced Physical Therapy (APT). I made an appointment and went for my first visit in July of 2008. It would turn out to be one of the best decisions I had ever made.

Advanced Physical Therapy - Valerie Gibson, PT, DPT

APT, is in Vienna, VA, about 2 miles from my house. I drove my car, a 2003 BMW to the appointment. I had purchased the car 5 years prior and I loved every minute I drove it. I was using a walker whenever I left the house. I had given up on using 2 canes due to my latest fall and because I needed the extra support. Of course, in my mind all of this was temporary. I would get some therapy and finally fix the physical decline that had happened over the last 5 years. One of my strong attributes is being stubborn and not accepting my situation but the same stubbornness currently in my life was causing me physical and mental problems. I was finally going to deal with my issues, at least the physical ones.

My first thoughts of APT was that it was much different than any other physical therapy center I had been in. There wasn't a receptionist to check in, so I sat down in the lobby area and within 5 minutes Valerie came over to me and introduced herself. I filled out a couple of forms and followed her back to a raised mat. At the time I was using a three wheeled walker. She said I should use a 4-wheeler because it would be much safer. Then she introduced me to everyone at therapy. Everybody said hi and I already felt welcomed. In my experience at other therapy facilities the people kept to themselves, so this place was a nice change. I felt like the new kid on my first day at school.

When I had initially talked to Valerie on the phone, I gave a short rundown of my current situation and medical history. During my appointment I gave more details about my recent physical troubles and what I was hoping to accomplish in therapy. Valerie gave me a thorough physical evaluation and at the end she discussed exercises and treatment that would help me. I asked a few questions and at the end of our talk, Valerie, probably seeing the stress on my face, said with a calm confidence not to worry and that things would get better. I felt a sense of relief that I hadn't felt in a long time and it took all my energy not to break down and cry. The physical problems I was having over the last few years were bad, and I was keeping it all inside. She had given me hope and that was what I needed right then.

I'm writing this part of the book in the Spring of 2017 and what I can remember about the time from July of 2008 to the Fall of 2011 is very uneventful in that I didn't make any trips or do anything that sticks out in my mind since I was continuing to physically deteriorate. I was going to therapy twice a week. I would use my walker to get to my car. I would leave the walker in the driveway and drive to therapy. When I got to therapy, I would call Valerie and her assistant, Carlos, would come out with a wheelchair and bring me in. Once there, I would use one of Valerie's walkers. APT has a wide range of equipment and I would use most of the machines to strengthen my arms and legs. Valerie would stretch my legs that were tight and spastic. Another chronic problem area was my lower back. The way I was walking was causing a lot of stress and pain. I was using an ice pack every evening along with pain medication. I was treating the symptoms but not the cause. But it was probably due to the way I struggled to walk and the way I was arching my back to lift my weakening legs.

Valerie suggested some additional treatments I could do outside of therapy. She suggested that I get Botox injections into my adductor muscle (inner thigh). The tightness of these muscles was making it difficult to walk and was causing me pain. I had the injections every three months for a couple of years, and it provided me some relief. During this time, I also was getting acupuncture treatments. Acupuncture is a form of alternative medicine in which very thin needles are inserted into the body. It's a key component of traditional Chinese medicine. It is most often used for pain relief, though it is also used for a wide range of other conditions. Acupuncture is generally used only in combination with other forms of treatment. I was hoping it would be an alternative to the pain medication I had been taking for 25 years. I was skeptical at first but after a couple of months of treatments I was getting substantial pain relief. The downside was the treatments aren't covered by insurance and were costing me $80 for each treatment which eventually caused me to stop the acupuncture sessions. After that I was getting bimonthly massages and to make it a little easier Valerie found me a masseuse that would come to my house. For those of you who have had a massage, you know how helpful it can be. It helps both physically and mentally and I looked forward to my treatments. I also went to a pain clinic and had a spinal block to stop the pain in my back, hip and leg. After two spinal blocks, there was no relief. Another dead end. I should add that Christine or Diane, or Tom had to drive me to most of these appointments because it was too far and painful for me to walk from the parking lot to the office.

During this time, I was trying everything I could to get better. In some ways it was helping, slowing down my physical decline and helping me deal with the pain and the depression that was slowly creeping in on me, but I was losing the battle. I was talking to my doctor and doing research on the internet. Valerie was trying everything she could think of and of course we were working hard in my therapy sessions. She would text me in the evenings to see how I was feeling or to find out about a treatment or doctor's appointment. Also, during this time, I rarely went out of the house. It was too difficult. My friends came to visit me at home which really helped.

In November of 2011, I searched for my "old friend" Dr. Cooney and found that he was part of a group of doctors that had formed The Washington Brain and Spine Institute. I was hoping that he could help me or find someone that could. I called and found out that he had retired a few months earlier. I figured I would see one of the other doctors in the practice, tell him my problems and hope I still had some options. My pain was constant, and my spasticity was increasing rapidly. I think that my spasticity was exacerbating my pain and vice versa. Over the last three months, I was struggling. In the morning I was having difficulty getting in and out of the shower and getting dressed. I was also missing therapy either because I was too tired to drive there or just didn't care about going.

As I've been saying, I was always trying to find anything, drugs, therapies, nerve blocks or acupuncture to help with pain. One drug that my physician suggested I try was Lyrica. Lyrica is prescribed mostly for neurological pain. It can treat a burning pain that some diabetic people can get in their feet. One of my worst pains was the burning pain I have in my feet. Sounds like a winner, right? I took this medication for over a year and never really had any pain relief. In fact, the side effects and there were a few bad ones, forced me to stop taking it. But with this medication you must slowly lower your dosage over time. I had withdrawal symptoms similar to being addicted to drugs but eventually I was able to get off it.

In November of 2011, my brother took me to the appointment I made with one of the doctors from the Brain and Spine Center in Bethesda. After the Neurologist examined me and listened to my problems, he thought I would be a good candidate for an intrathecal pump. An intrathecal pump system consists of a pump/reservoir implanted between the muscle and skin of your abdomen and a catheter that carries pain medication from the pump to the spinal cord and nerves. The pump is programmed to slowly release medication over a period of time. A combination of pain medication and Baclofen for spasticity would be used. I had talked to a few people that had Baclofen pumps and were satisfied with the system. I agreed to do it and set up an appointment in late January. The pump would be tried externally at first to see if it worked and if it was successful it would be implanted. I would have the procedure done over a three-day time period at Suburban Hospital.

Suburban Hospital, January 2012

I checked into my hospital room the morning of January 17, 2012. I sat around until the afternoon until I finally saw a doctor. He would give me my epidural. At the last minute my doctor decided that the best thing to do was to give me a morphine epidural because getting rid of my pain was more important than reducing my spasticity. It sounded right at the time, but I didn't have any time to think about it. I sat at the edge of my bed and the doctor inserted the needle. I have been through a lot but the pain from getting that needle inserted into my spine was right up there. Eventually after pushing and reinserting, the doctor finally got it in the correct place in my spine. The morphine drip started and soon I wasn't feeling any pain. Also, all the spasticity had gone out of my legs. It was about 3 o'clock. I was standing by my bed and walking around the room soon after the epidural but as the evening wore on it was getting harder to stand. I lay in bed all evening and by 11 o'clock, I had another problem. I hadn't peed since before the procedure, which was becoming a problem. By midnight I was in pain and I had to be catheterized. Because I was unable to walk or pee, the next morning the doctor and I agreed to stop the procedure. The epidural was removed, and I was assured that as soon as the morphine cleared my system, I would regain both functions. By mid-morning, I still couldn't pee or stand. I would spend another night in the hospital. By the next morning I still couldn't stand, and my legs were very weak, but I was finally able to pee. I was released from the hospital and went home in a wheelchair. This whole epidural trial had been a disaster. I was trying anything that would help but it looked like I had run out of options which was not something I could accept but it was looking like I finally might have to.

I needed to get home health care until I could walk. The morphine was out of my system. I could stand but I couldn't take any steps. I called a company that provided in-home certified nursing assistants (CNA). I would need help getting out of bed, showering and getting dressed. I was hoping it would be only for a couple of days. They sent a nice man named Ibrahim. Over a one-week period he helped me each day until the last day when I was able to do everything by myself. I had dodged another bullet, but I was right back in the same bad situation I was in before this fiasco.

In early February, I was having difficulty getting out of bed some mornings due to lightheadedness. I would have to call to my sister to help me stand up. Once I got up, I could get into the shower but some days I nearly fell and getting dressed left me exhausted. Other days were better, it was hit or miss. During the nights I wasn't sleeping well. I had pain in my legs and spasms that woke me up. I couldn't safely get to the bathroom during the night, so I started using a bedside urinal. During the month of February, I was having 3 to 4 bad days a week. Always in pain, frustrated, angry at myself and was becoming a burden to my family especially to my sister Diane. I had always found a way out of bad situations, but it was getting clearer to me there wasn't a way out of this one. One evening things got so bad that I had to be taken to the emergency room. I was in extreme pain and frustrated and basically having a panic attack. I'm not trying to be dramatic, but there were a few times during these horrible months, that I contemplated suicide. I was becoming a burden to my family and my quality of life was poor and getting worse. I was 51 and couldn't imagine living like this for the rest of my life. Looking back now, this was my rock bottom. But just as soon as that thinking came into my head, I knew it wasn't an option. I would sit down and cry, take a deep breath and do my best to regroup. On one occasion, when I broke down, something amazing happened. Sensing my pain and despair, Boomer came right over to me and sat down right in front of me and looked at me with his big brown eyes and basically "said" what can I do to help you? Maybe he was thinking it would be nice if you rolled yourself over and got me a treat. Whatever happened that day, Boomer seemed to know when I needed a friend. From then on, he followed me wherever I went to make sure I was ok. If he heard me yell or scream in my bedroom, he came right in to see if I was ok. It was sure good to have him with me during those dark days.

I was missing more therapy appointments, so I arranged to have a guy drive me to therapy and take me home. He had been a helper to one of Valerie's patients and was not working at the time. He showed up Monday on time and Wednesday too. On Friday I had him drive me to the bank, so I could pay him cash. He asked to borrow $100 dollars and I gave it to him because I would be paying him that each week. I waited and waited for him on the following Monday morning, but he never showed up. He took the money and ran.

During this 6 to 9 month decline, Valerie was doing everything she could to help me in and out of therapy. She could see my frustration and most likely my change in attitude. She would check on me at home through texts or phone calls and would sometimes just let me vent my frustration to her. She knew I was having difficulty getting ready in the morning and suggested I call for a CNA to help me get dressed and drive me to therapy. I was spending many days just sitting in my chair staring at the TV getting more depressed and she knew I needed to get out of the house and get back to therapy.

After dragging my feet, I called the same agency I used in January and after describing what I needed, I asked if Ibrahim was available. He was so helpful, and I was comfortable with him, but he was working with another person. The woman suggested another CNA named Abu Sesay who she described as one of their best. I agreed, and Abu came to help me in late March 2012. At first, I only wanted him for 3 days a week. In my thinking I would be ok on my own on non-therapy days. I learned quickly that I would need him every day. There were days that I could just barely get showered and dressed on my own: other days I needed help. I never knew what the day would be like until I woke up. So, I hired Abu for 4 hours every day. He would help me get dressed and get breakfast and then he would drive me to therapy 2 or 3 times a week. He drove me to my doctor's appointments and stayed with me until Diane came home for lunch. The rest of the afternoon I would just sit and watch TV, only walking to the bathroom and back. There were a couple of times that I fell on the floor when I was alone and had to call Diane at work. She would have to leave work and somehow, she was able to get me back on my feet.

One morning while Abu was with me, I was standing by the sink in my kitchen when I had a violent spasm. My spasticity was also getting worse. The back of my head hit the upper kitchen cabinet causing my legs to go numb. Abu barely caught me before I hit the ground. Because of the temporary loss of feeling in my legs, I reluctantly, after talking to Valerie, called 911 and was taken on a stretcher to the hospital. I called Diane at work and she followed the ambulance in her car and Tom met us there. I was in the emergency room for 5 hours and released after being checked out by the doctor. I had gotten my feeling back in my legs. Another adventure in the books.

Spasticity

Clinically, spasticity results from the loss of inhibition of motor neurons, causing excessive velocity-dependent muscle contraction. This ultimately leads to hyperreflexia, an exaggerated deep tendon reflex. Spasticity is often treated with the drug baclofen which I take daily. The cause of spasticity is not really known, but there are several theories. One factor that is thought to be related to spasticity is the stretch reflex. This reflex is important in coordinating normal movements in which muscles are contracted and relaxed and in keeping the muscle from stretching too far. Although the result of spasticity is problems with the muscles, spasticity is caused by an injury to a part of the central nervous system (the brain or spinal cord) that controls voluntary movements.

The damage causes a change in the balance of signals between the nervous system and the muscles. This imbalance leads to increased activity (excitability) in the muscles. Receptors in the muscles receive messages from the nervous system, which sense the amount of stretch in the muscle and sends that signal to the brain. The brain responds by sending a message back to reverse the stretch by contracting or shortening.

My spasticity ranges from minimal to moderate. If I stay in the same position for too long, like being in bed all night my spasticity is bad. But getting into a warm shower can help greatly. If I'm working out, which I do at least 5 days a week it's very minimal and it can last for a couple of hours after my workout. I take Baclofen every three hours to lessen the effects of the spasticity. Some of the benefits I get from my spasticity is that the random spasms help keep tone in my leg muscles that get little movement and I can strategically use a spasm by triggering it to help me stand at therapy, move my leg if I need to or even roll over in bed. I've learned to live with it but at times it can be very frustrating.

In late March, I made another appointment with my doctor at the Brain and Spine Center in Bethesda to review what had happened or didn't happen with the pain pump procedure at the hospital in January. Tom took me. I was also still looking for anything that would help with my terrible pain and increasing spasticity. It was a last desperate try. During the discussion we were talking about my pain symptoms again and I mentioned that when I turned my head hard to the right my left arm would tingle and get numb. I told him this had been happening for a few years. I described other major symptoms I had, including an increasing weakness in my legs, loss of balance and terrible back pain and a change in urinary function, both incontinence and retention. He said that these were symptoms of a tethered spinal cord. That most likely was due to the fracture and dislocation of my neck in 1977 and the subsequent increase of scar tissue, from my surgery in my cervical spine over the years. My spinal cord could have grown to or "tethered" to my spine. I finally felt like I had found a viable reason why I had been physically deteriorating over the last 5 to 7 years. I asked him what my options were to address this issue.

Post-traumatic Tethered Spinal Cord

Post-traumatic tethered spinal cord is a condition which may occur following injury to the spinal cord where scar tissue forms and tethers or holds the spinal cord to the soft tissue covering which surrounds it called the dura. This scar tissue prevents the normal flow of spinal fluid around the spinal cord and impedes the normal motion of the spinal cord.

The onset of new pains or the worsening of pains that were present at the time of injury may occur. Secondary to these pains, patients report various types of symptoms, including burning, stinging, stabbing, sharp, shooting, electrical, crushing, squeezing, tight, vise-like cramping pains. These pains generally occur in areas where patients have lost sensation or where sensation sense is not normal. I had many of these symptoms and my condition was getting worse by the week.

My doctor at the Brain and Spine center knew of a neurosurgeon at The National Institute of Health (NIH) in Bethesda, Maryland who had an open clinical trial working with people dealing with Tethered Cord disorders. I called and applied to be part of the clinical trial. Part of the process was completing an extensive application, including medical history and an examination. My physical exam was scheduled for the last week in April. I asked Tom and Suzy to come with me to ask questions and listen to the doctor. I strongly advise you to bring someone with you to listen to the doctor's feedback and proposed treatments for important visits like this one. If you are stressed during your visit you may not remember everything said or maybe stop listening after a potential bad diagnosis is talked about and not hear the positive treatments.

My appointment was at 10 am and we were taken to the exam room right on time. The whole feeling when you're at NIH is different than any other medical facility I had ever been to. Many years earlier when my dad had been successfully treated there, I was amazed at his doctors and nurses' care. I was to meet with Dr. John Heiss. At the time, Dr. Heiss was the Chairman of the Surgical Neurology Branch at NIH. He came in a few minutes later with two other doctors who were part of his team working with the tethered cord clinical trial. He had my detailed medical history and an MRI that I had done in December. I talked for a while giving him and his team details of my past injury (1977) and recovery and then spent more time talking about the last 6 to 9 months when my condition was deteriorating much faster. This took a little while, but it was information they needed. He and his colleagues asked questions and we talked for a while. Like all other doctor's appointments I had before, I figured I didn't have much time to discuss my problem, but he assured me that we had as much time as I needed. I had a good first impression of him. Next came the physical exam. One of the other doctors performed the exam while the other one took notes. Dr. Heiss was asking them questions as they progressed. They seemed to be medical students or interns. Then we all went to a room to view my MRI on a large computer screen. He explained what we were seeing and talked about the original injury and the damage to my vertebrae. He traced my spinal cord and showed us where my spinal column was narrow and then he pointed out where my spinal cord had tethered to the dura from approximately C-4 to C-7 or even L-1. Looking at the MRI, I could see the normal width of the spinal column, but through the original damaged area the cord area was so thin. I was amazed at how I was able to function so well over the years with the cord being squeezed through that area. The doctor was positive that it was tethered, and it was most likely the cause of my decline. He was unsure how long it had been tethered or when it started. We all went back to the exam room to discuss my options.

Dr. Heiss described the surgery to de-tether or detach my spinal cord from my spine. The surgery involves removing bone in the back of the neck to get to the dura- the covering around the spinal cord. He would use ultrasound to identify the area of scar tissue formation and then open the dura and release the bands of scar tissue to restore spinal fluid flow and motion of the spinal cord. The dura would be closed using an expansion duraplasty- a graft placed to enhance the dural space and decrease the risk of re-scarring. In my case he would use a piece of bovine pericardium (cow's heart) as the graft. If my spinal cord didn't re-tether in the first 6 months following surgery, then it would most likely not be a problem for me in the future.

He then explained to me the potential outcomes following surgery. First, there was a small chance that the surgery might improve my situation. Second, there was a chance that the surgery could make things worse due to the process of detaching the cord, additional nerves could be damaged. The third option was to fully detach the cord and stop my physical deterioration without causing any further damage. This was the most likely outcome. I then asked him what he would suggest I do, and he hesitated to give me a clear answer. He wanted me to decide. Then I said to him I have a tethered cord and it needs to be fixed or I'm going to get worse and he said "yes". So, I said I wanted to do the surgery. We finished the discussion and he sent me to his assistant to set up a date for the surgery. I was excited at the fact that after all these years I finally had found a cause for my problems and I was going to have a chance to fix it. Dr. Heiss had made me aware of the downside of the surgery but where I was at this point in my life, I really didn't have any other options.

I met with the surgery scheduler and in the back of my mind I figured I would have at least 6 weeks to wait until she could fit me into his surgery schedule, but she surprised me and said, "how about May 15th?" That was only 2 weeks away. I didn't say anything. Then she said the next opening he had was in early June. I noted the dates and said I would need to think about it, and I would call her back. I was tired and overwhelmed by the whole day. I needed to go home and regroup. Tom drove me home and my mind was grinding over the decision. I talked over a few things from the meeting with him and then one thing suddenly hit me. If I didn't take the May 15th date, I would have to wait another 6 weeks. That meant more pain and suffering. My reluctance was that I needed to be ready mentally for the surgery. That was always how I dealt with prior medical procedures, but I wouldn't have that luxury this time. It was sooner than I was ready for, but I had to reserve that date. As soon as I got home, I called back and scheduled my surgery for the 15th.

Meanwhile, I knew that after the surgery and short stay at NIH, I would need to go to a rehab facility. Suzy came through for me by researching the rehab hospitals in the area. One hospital I asked her to check out was Shady Grove Adventist in Rockville. During my hours of internet researching treatments for spasticity, I came across Shady Grove and Dr. Terrence Sheehan. Suzy went to talk to the hospital administrators and took a tour of the facility. She had told them my situation and they seemed genuinely excited for me to rehab there. One of the administrators there had been involved in Christopher Reeves rehabilitation following his spinal cord injury.

The two weeks before the surgery I was extra careful. Abu would help me get showered and dressed each morning. I would spend the rest of the day in my lift chair. I knew if I accidentally fell and was injured it would jeopardize my scheduled surgery. Diane did the rest by coming home from work at lunchtime and making me dinner. Every night Diane, Tom or my neighbor Jeff or my friend Shali, would help me get into bed. All of us just trying to get me to the 15th. The one thing I did accomplish prior to my surgery, was getting my living will completed. I also wrote a detailed will. Like most people I had put off doing this but knowing how serious the surgery was it was time to get it done.

The National Institutes of Health

Bethesda, MD

I arrived at NIH the day before the surgery. Abu drove me, and we met Suzy there and got checked in. I got to my room midday and had an MRI in the evening. By then Abu and Suzy had gone home and Tom was with me. I've had several MRI's and I don't like them. I usually tough it out but this time I took two Valium. No problem. Then it was back to my room. I don't remember sleeping much that night waiting for my 7am surgery.

Tuesday morning, May 15th. The surgical nurses and techs came and got me at 6am. They transferred me to a gurney and took me to the surgical waiting room where I signed a lot of forms and met the surgical staff and a brief meeting with Dr. Heiss. Tom, Suzy and Christine were with me until they took me to the operating room. We had decided the night before that I would see them all after the surgery but all three of them were there at 6am. What an amazing family I have. After 10 hours of surgery, I woke up in my hospital room paralyzed from the neck down. Here we go again. This time I was in my own room, no traction, I had some sensory feeling, but I was unable to move at all. I knew this was a possibility, and I mentally tried to prepare myself for it, but nothing you can do can make you able to deal with being paralyzed, especially for a second time.

From what I later read about the surgery, Dr. Heiss made an incision from C2 to T1. Because of the 1977 laminectomy, there wasn't much bone to cut through. He then began the long process of detaching my spinal cord from the dura without damaging the spinal cord and causing me any additional physical harm. He wrote in his notes, that I read later, that at C7 he was unable to fully free the cord, so part of the cord is still attached there. The benefit from the surgery was always to alleviate my excruciating pain and debilitating spasticity. I knew the risks going into the procedure and here I was again lying in bed totally paralyzed. A couple of hours after I was awake, Dr. Heiss told me he was very happy with how things went, and he was confident that some feeling would return. He said I could start my rehab when I was ready. I didn't have any restrictions on my neck movement. I didn't have a spinal fusion with rods or screws. I had to be careful of my incision. I had my old friend the catheter back, but I hoped to get rid of that soon. I knew my condition was worse from the surgery. I couldn't move my legs at all, and my arms and hands had little movement. I hoped it was temporary. I wasn't too upset or panicked because I'd been in this situation before and I was just cocky enough to think I could recover again.

My family was there when I woke up and heard Dr. Heise's post-surgery comments. I had my own room and the nursing staff was excellent. My experience at NIH was awesome. From my initial evaluation to my discharge 6 days later. We are so lucky as a country to have this facility available to us and for the amazing research that is being done there.

My friend Carole came from California to visit me on Wednesday, the day after surgery. I've known Carole for over 20 years. I mentioned that we worked together for about seven years, but we have been close friends ever since. She had just graduated from nursing school a few days earlier and flew to help me as soon as she could. She asked the staff if she could stay in my room overnight to help me and they said she could. Her presence during those nights was so helpful. Getting me anything I needed or finding a nurse to get my pain medication on time. She stayed 4 nights and made things bearable when I was most vulnerable. I'll never be able to thank her enough. With my family visiting during the days and Carole watching my back during the night, I felt as comfortable as I could. My amazing support system was in full control.

Since I was not flat on my back for too long, I could transfer to a wheelchair and be taken to the therapy room on the third day following surgery. I was able to have my legs moved and stretched a little. This was a whole lot different than my first few days at Suburban hospital in 1977. My injury was evaluated by the therapist using the ASIA scale as all spinal cord injured patients are.

The ASIA scale is a system of tests used to define and describe the extent and severity of a patient's spinal cord injury and help determine future rehabilitation and recovery needs. It is ideally completed within 72 hours after the initial injury. The patient's grade is based on how much sensation he or she can feel at multiple points on the body, as well as tests of motor function.

ASIA Impairment Scale

Grade A-Complete lack of motor and sensory function below the level of injury (including the anal area)

Grade B-Some sensation below the level of the injury (including anal sensation)

Grade C-Some muscle movement is spared below the level of injury, but 50 percent of the muscles below the level of injury cannot move against gravity.

Grade D-Most (more than 50 percent) of the muscles that are spared below the level of injury are strong enough to move against gravity.

Grade E-All neurologic function has returned.

I was graded a B. I was not happy with my post-surgical prognosis. But I was not surprised. I was aware of the dangers. I would have fit into a Grade D before surgery. But being able to get out of bed so quickly and doing a little therapy two days post-surgery was impressive if I do say so. I had to focus on my rehab and forget about the past. Keeping that mindset for the last 35 years has kept me from playing the "what if" game. I knew I would only be there for a few days before I would be transferred to Shady Grove for more intensive rehab. After a few days I was able to trade in the internal catheter for an external Texas catheter and a couple of weeks after that I would be catheter free. The surgery had made me temporarily incontinent. This in addition to my paralysis were big setbacks but I wasn't upset. I was confident, at that point, that both issues would be temporary. My spinal cord was 95% free and spinal fluid was surrounding it as it should be. That was positive, but I could have serious problems such as autonomic dysreflexia.

Autonomic Dysreflexia (AD), also known as Hyperreflexia, is a potentially dangerous complication of a spinal cord injury (SCI). In AD, an individual's blood pressure may rise to dangerous levels and if not treated can lead to stroke and possibly death. Individuals with SCI at the T-6 level or above are at greater risk.

I had experience with being paralyzed and recovering from it. I knew I would I just needed to work hard and hopefully I would be in a much better position than I was prior to the surgery, where the pain and spasticity were unbearable. Dr. Heiss said that patients can make physical improvements for up to 12 months, but most patients don't improve after that. I of course, didn't think these statistics applied to me. That might sound cocky or unrealistic but that is how I think. I looked at my predicament like I was just rehabbing from an injury. I knew it will take time but as long as I continued to make progress my thinking would continue to be the same. For me, there isn't any other way to look at it. I don't have a disease so why shouldn't I get better. It might take time, but I am patient. Now, as I continue to rehab, I try to find any improvements and if there are, that keeps me going.

During the week I was there, Dr. Heiss checked up on me daily and each time he had another doctor with him. Some of these doctors were from the US, but most were visiting from many different countries. I was examined and asked a lot of questions. Some doctors had translators. I found this fascinating and I would do anything to help further their research. The surgery and care for the past week were priceless to me and as part of the study I would be available if they needed me.

Shady Grove Adventist Rehabilitation Hospital

On May 21, 2012, I said goodbye to the NIH staff and took a 30-minute ambulance ride to Shady Grove Rehabilitation. It would be a new adventure for me. After the first injury I stayed in the same hospital for my entire rehab. The goal here would be to get me physically able to safely transition back home. I checked into my room on the second floor. Tom met me there to make sure I got settled in. The two-story rehab facility has 53 beds and is adjacent to Shady Grove Hospital. It specializes in the treatment of traumatic brain injuries, amputations, spinal cord injuries and strokes. Dr. Terrence Sheehan is the (CMO) Chief Medical Officer and is board certified in spinal cord injuries. He oversaw my case. Later that day I met him, and he explained my daily rehab schedule. They weren't messing around there. I had 2 one-hour physical therapy sessions and one hour of occupational therapy each day. Other than 45 minutes for lunch, I had some scheduled treatment until 3 o'clock each day. They don't want you lying in your room. I went to group meetings once a day with hospital personnel talking about coping with your injury. I attended these meetings for a few days, but they were more depressing to me than helpful. I understand their purpose and I know they are helpful to many patients, but I've developed my own set of coping skills over the last 35 years. I was given a power wheelchair the next day to get around on my own and it gave me some independence after I learned to use it. Dr. Sheehan removed the stitches on the back of my neck and a leftover staple from my temple. During surgery my head was secured with a neurosurgical head holder (skull clamp) system. This is a device used to secure the patient's head position during surgical procedures.

My day started anytime between 6:30 and 8 am depending on when the nursing staff gave me my bed bath and got me dressed. I had very minimal movement in my arms and none in my legs. My first therapy was usually at 8 am and I was late a few mornings. My physical therapist was Angie Owens. She was 5 months pregnant and one of the most smart and amazing people I had ever met. When I was not on time in the morning, she was in my room looking for me and trying to figure out what I needed to get to the therapy room. There were days that she transferred me from my bed to my chair by herself instead of waiting for another male staff member to do it. At Shady Grove the therapy facility is on the same floor as all the patient's rooms. It was my first day at therapy. I had a quick breakfast in my room, and I needed to be transferred to my chair. I hadn't completely gotten over being lightheaded when I was sitting fully upright. I was taking medication to raise my blood pressure, but I also must be careful to avoid autonomic dysreflexia. There was a sign above my bed for all the hospital staff to be aware of this issue. I was still using a Texas catheter which slightly hindered my therapy.

The nursing staff transferred me to my chair, and I went down the hall to PT. It was the first day of school and I was the new kid. As I rolled into the large room, I got the once over from a few of the patients exercising. Each therapy session was either 60 or 90 minutes with a break in between. Angie gave me a brief overview of what we needed to accomplish before I could be released. The therapy sessions the first week were very rudimentary. Angie was evaluating my level of injury and how she could help me. My days were tightly scheduled. By 3 or 4 o'clock I was finished for the day.

I had the nursing staff to transfer me back into bed and I usually took a 30-minute nap. Every night I got a menu of meals for the next day. The food there was ok but let's be honest, it was hospital food. My family members live 20-30 minutes away from Shady Grove but one of them brought me dinner every night from a nearby restaurant. There are a few fast food places and a couple of good restaurants directly across the street from the hospital. They got menus and we had dinner together. It was the highlight of my day. Tom, Christine and Suzy handled most of the weekdays and Diane visited me on the weekends which was nice because I didn't have therapy. She even brought our dog Boomer up for a long visit. My Uncle Chick visited a few afternoons each week and my friends stopped by too. Marian, who lives in Delaware, came to visit on weekends. Since it was the summer Katy, Thomas and Megan occasionally brought me lunch during the week. It was such a mental boost to have them stop by. My family isn't the touchy feely type. We aren't too affectionate with each other. I don't know why, and I don't really care to figure it out. But I will tell you this for sure, if any one of us needs help, and a lot of the time it's me, they drop everything and are right there ready to help. Like a well-oiled machine. They will organize and purchase and make calls and show up anytime and anywhere you need them and when the job is done and when the need is over everyone goes back to their own lives until the next phone call. It's an unmatched support system and I don't know where I would be without them.

Christine, Marian and Diane

Suzy and Tom

The nights in the hospital were difficult as I remember. I had a few roommates, and a few had suffered severe strokes and couldn't communicate very well, if at all. I couldn't imagine not being able to talk to the nurse and tell them that you need a blanket, medication or even a drink of water. Even though I was in rough shape, compared to them, I had no reason to complain. I can't move too well but everything else is working and my support system is excellent. Still, it was noisy and lights from the hallway were distracting. Nurses were coming and going in my room in the middle of the night. When the 7 am shift came on duty they were getting supplies from the room next to me. The heavy metal door slammed over and over. Unable to move, I had to press my call button to get somebody to help me turn from one side to the other. Shady Grove is one of the best facilities I've been in but the six weeks I was there were tough, and they took a toll on me. When I wasn't in therapy, I would go outside in my chair and just sit in the sun or ride around the hospital grounds which was nice.

In therapy, we were working on transferring me from my chair to a raised mat. I was working on improving the strength and dexterity of my fingers in occupational therapy. How to use a fork and knife, put on a shirt etc. A few weeks in, Abu visited me, and I was hoping he would help me full time when I got home. Lucky for me he said he would. Angie wanted him to come back and learn how to transfer me from a wheelchair to my car. Valerie also visited me one night and she brought subs for dinner. I updated her on my condition. She did a quick evaluation and we had a nice visit. When I got home, I would have in-home therapy for a couple of weeks before going back to Valerie's therapy center (APT). But I had a long way to go before I would get back there.

One day in the early afternoon, a hospital staff member told me that there was a slight miscommunication with my brother. It seemed there was another patient named Brown who had a stroke and the hospital staff mixed up the two Browns. The person at the desk had called my brother at his office and said that I had had a stroke. Tom left work in DC and was speeding up interstate 270 to check on me. He knew that due to my autonomic dysreflexia, a stroke was possible. When they told me about the mix up, I called Tom on his cellphone. He answered on his way up and said he just got a call from the hospital to explain the mistake. Tom was fired up and I don't blame him. He wanted to know how a mistake like this could be made. He stopped by my room to see me and I tried to calm him down, but he was furious. He talked to Dr. Sheehan and some staff members. I could hear his voice from the nurse's station. We would discuss it later at our weekly family update meeting. I had a few department managers visit me each day and promise to get me anything I needed, which made things a little better. Every day after that mix up it seemed like some hospital staff member checked on me.

I was working hard in therapy, but I didn't feel I was making any progress. The surgery had paralyzed me again and I wasn't pulling off another miracle. Not even close. I guess it's one to a customer. At the end of every week I had a meeting with Dr. Sheehan, Angie, my occupational therapist, and any of my family members who might be with me that day. We discussed my progress and as the weeks went on, we talked about my discharge date. In mid-June, it looked like if I continued my progress, I could go home on June 22nd. Dr. Sheehan arranged for me to go home for a few hours one day. I got a handicap cab to pick me up one morning and take me home. Tom came up to the hospital and followed me back home. I had purchased a ramp to get up the one step into my house through my porch door. I spent about 5 hours home before returning to the hospital. It was nice to get away and most of my family was there. Boomer, too. I went back to Shady Grove in the afternoon. I only had 10 days left before I would get discharged. I was counting the days.

One thing we needed to work on before I could go home, was transferring from my wheelchair to my car. Tom and Abu met Angie and I in the hospital parking lot and after a few tries we worked it out. I also needed to have a home evaluation. They wanted to make sure my house was suitable for me and my wheelchair. I live in a one level home. I never thought that one day I would need a one level house, but it paid off. Two therapists and I traveled back to my house a few days before I was released from the hospital. They made sure I had access into my house via a ramp and that I could get around my house in my wheelchair. I was using a loner power chair that I got from the hospital. A couple of weeks into my stay in the hospital, I was measured for my own wheelchair that I would get a couple of months later. They checked my bed and my bathroom and knowing that Abu will be helping me in the mornings I got approved to come home on June 22nd. With the home inspection completed, we all headed back to the hospital.

All in all, my time at Shady Grove wasn't too bad. As good as a hospital stay could be. There wasn't any privacy and you never got a decent night of sleep. My family came through for me, as usual, with timely visits to keep my spirits high. The visits from my friends including Valerie, Abu, Jerry, Carrie, Jeff and Uncle Chick were great. Shawn was able to make it up from Charlotte for a visit. I was able to complete the necessary tasks in therapy to be released. I was not happy with my physical situation. I was confined to a wheelchair and I hadn't made any progress getting back on my feet. I had in-home therapy for a couple of weeks and then I would go back to Valerie's where we could focus on improving my overall condition. On the 22nd, my brother came to help me check out. We packed all my stuff and I stopped to say goodbye to my therapist Angie. It would have been very difficult to have survived here without her. Her therapy plan was wonderful, but she also got me through the down times, which were many. I was lucky to have Dr. Sheehan in charge of my rehab. He's extremely kind and knowledgeable and I see him every six months to keep him up to date on my rehab and what's going on in my life. I still have a weird feeling every time I go back there. Anyway, I left the hospital with no fanfare, patients come and go here all the time. Tom packed my things in his trunk, and I got in the wheelchair van, and we headed back home to Beulah Beach.

It obviously felt good to be home. Diane brought my stuff in and my rehab stint was complete. I had to adjust to my house, my bathroom and bed without round the clock nursing staff. At night I had to transfer from my chair to the bed, get my medication, use a bedside urinal, and turn myself side to side. The first couple of weeks were very stressful but with the help of my in-home occupational therapist I got my bed situation worked out. I was constantly thinking of how to make things easier, searching the internet or asking people for their help. Diane was able to help me transfer to my bed. I continued with in-home therapy for 2 weeks and then returned to Valerie's. On the evening of June 29th, a week after being home, a severe storm knocked the power out in Vienna. The June 2012 Mid-Atlantic and Midwest derecho was one of the most destructive and deadly fast-moving severe thunderstorm complexes in North American history.

The progressive derecho tracked across a large section of the Midwestern United States and across the central Appalachians into the mid-Atlantic states on the afternoon and evening of June 29, 2012, and into the early morning of June 30, 2012. It resulted in a total of 22 deaths, millions of power outages across the entire affected region, and a damage total of US $2.9 billion exceeded that of all but the top 25 Atlantic tropical cyclones.

The storm hit my house hard, the wind tore the screen off my kitchen door and blew down a huge cedar tree in my front yard that just missed hitting our cars. The power went out. In the 20 years I've lived here, the few power outages I've had, only lasted a couple of hours. I live so close to the stores and restaurants in the town, that outages don't last long. But this time would be different. We were without power for almost 4 days and the storm didn't bring a break in the heat, in fact it got hotter. I don't know how I would have made it without Diane. She put ice packs on me throughout the night. Abu came in the morning, as usual, and I took long cold showers. I didn't have any other place to go, because there was no power anywhere the first 2 days and staying in my house with my bed were as good as anywhere else I could go. Anyway, I was confident that the power would come on soon. It always did.

The nights were the worst. Temps inside the house were in the upper 80's and with my autonomic nerve damage, one of my problems was that I didn't sweat and that could lead to other serious problems. On the second day, Diane called 911, because I was having chest pains. I was checked out and Diane went to the firehouse to fill up a cooler with ice. On day three, I took a wheelchair taxi to spend the day at the Vienna Community Center, because they finally had power restored and air conditioning. During the afternoon of the fourth day, when I was physically and mentally done, the power finally came back on. I guess it would have been better to have stayed in the hospital one more week.

After "normalcy" was restored, I was getting better adjusted to being home. Abu got me ready in the morning and Diane was able to transfer me into my bed. Christine, who spent a few days a week with us also learned how to transfer me and Tom and my neighbors Jeff Erhardt and Shali Tennakoon helped too. I've known Jeff for over 10 years since we met while I was working at a mortgage company. He has helped me out on many occasions as well as done more than a few repairs at Beulah Beach but mostly he's a good friend. I met Shali while working at Reilly Mortgage. He too, has become a close friend. He lives close by and will pretty much drop what he's doing and come to help. I finished my in-home therapy and I was very glad to be returning to therapy at Valerie's. Things were getting somewhat back to normal after a wild 10 weeks. I had a difficult road in front of me, but the surgery and hospital rehab were behind me. I found myself sometimes second guessing my decision to have the surgery considering my current condition, but I know it was the right call. The only option. When I think back to how bad I was physically, the six weeks leading up to the surgery, I really had no choice, but the thought has crept into my mind every now and then.

In early September as the weather cooled off, I wanted to have an end of Summer party, not a Beulah Beach blowout, just a get together for family and friends and the many people I hadn't seen since I was in the hospital. I also wanted to reconnect with friends I hadn't talked to for the few years since I had been homebound. News of my recent problems and surgery at NIH had travelled through the grapevine but the facts of the story can get lost or embellished. There's nothing better than to see someone face to face. While I was talking with some at the party, it seemed to me they were expecting to see me in a bad condition. I heard "You look great!" a few times. I don't know what they were expecting but it was nice to see everyone and show them that I was going to be ok. At the time, I was going back and forth to PT in the passenger seat of my BMW. I knew I had to get a wheelchair van of my own because it's way too difficult for Abu and me to do these transfers. I was also using wheelchair taxis to go to other appointments when Abu wasn't working with me which was expensive. I had worked through many things since I had been home, and the van was next on the list. In late September of 2012, I finally got my own power chair, and returned my loaner chair back to Shady Grove. The new chair allowed me to recline partially or fully and to raise the chair to reach things higher up and transfer into bed. I was spending about 12 hours in the chair and 12 hours in bed. Every morning I couldn't wait to get out of bed and every evening I couldn't wait to get out of the chair. It was a big adjustment being in a chair all day. It was as difficult as I could imagine. When it's time for me to transfer into bed, I'm really tired and in a lot of pain. It's important that I focus because I have to physically help my sister during the transfer and even though I've done it hundreds of times, I'm still nervous about falling. During the day, I had to be careful to recline periodically to avoid pressure sores. I sometimes transferred out of the chair at therapy which was nice. The interesting thing I was starting to learn was the amount of freedom and independence I had with the chair.

In August, I found a 2007 Dodge Grand Caravan online that had 27,000 miles on it. Some handicap vans are converted mini vans. The floors are lowered, and automatic ramps are added to allow access from the side door. But these vans, new or used, are not cheap. The blue book value of the van was $14,000; the handicap conversion was $16,000. I withdrew money from my IRA and bought the van for $30K. I was very lucky to find a nice used van with such low mileage. In general, being handicapped can be very expensive. Manual wheelchairs can be $500 and power wheelchairs can run from $15,000 upwards to $50,000 depending on the features. Insurance covers 50-80%. Scooters, walkers, canes, braces and orthotics can also be very expensive. Then there is home care help that averages $20- $30 an hour and the enormous cost of retrofitting your home. There's also the cost of physical therapy sessions. You might have to build or buy ramps and remodel bathrooms if you're lucky enough to be able to stay in your home. Some families must buy a stairlift to get up to their second-floor bedroom. Individuals and families must endure all these expenses with the probability of not being able to work for a while or ever. The financial burden is difficult at a time when you are trying to recover from your medical problem. It's very stressful for everyone.

Anyway, back to the van. I was able to ride my chair into the van and could be driven by Abu or anyone, to therapy, the store or anywhere I needed to go. The chair and the van would allow me the ability to do many things I hadn't done in many years. Kind of ironic. I took trips to the grocery store with Abu and that was great. Diane had been shopping for us for years but then I could look around the store and buy things for myself and give her a break.

On days I didn't go to therapy, Abu and I took short trips, to the mall, to the sporting goods store or to lunch. These usually mundane trips for most people were exciting new adventures for me. For 2 to 3 years prior to my surgery, I could drive to places but only walk very short distances with my walker. All of these trips were new to me and being out of the house made a big difference in my overall attitude. At the end of September, Shawn came for a visit and we went to a Washington Nationals game. I liked the freedom the van had given me. I settled into a pattern of going to therapy 2 to 3 times a week. I was working on overall strengthening. I was riding an arm and leg bike and standing in the parallel bars. Abu and Carlos helped me stand and supported me. As long as I kept my knees locked, I was ok, but my supported stands only lasted for 15 to 20 seconds before my legs gave out. Carlos has worked for Valerie for many years. The two of them run the whole business. Carlos is a therapy tech, computer guru, photographer, patient scheduler and equipment repairman to name a few jobs. He has helped me in more ways that I can name, and I am glad to have him as a friend.

As Christmas of 2012 neared, I got an idea in the middle of the night (usually when I get my best ideas) to do a Christmas card video. I could send the video to everyone and show them how I was doing in the 5 months since I left the rehab hospital. Carlos videoed me coming out of my van, working out on machines and at the end I was able to take a few assisted steps in the parallel bars all while Nat "King" Cole's The Christmas Song played in the background. Carlos did a great job editing the video. I sent the video to friends and family and Angie, Dr. Heiss and Dr. Sheehan, among the other people that had helped me through the surgery and rehab. I think it's still on YouTube. After viewing the video, Dr. Heise sent this response to me:

I wish Mr. Brown well with his efforts to rehabilitate his spinal cord injury. He looks like he is making progress. His eventual recovery will depend on him maximizing the function of the neurons that pass through the area of his spinal cord injury.

Hopefully new therapeutic strategies will be developed for patients with spinal cord injury that enable the neurons above the level of the spinal cord injury to penetrate the scar that occurs after spinal cord injury, extend their neuronal processes to re-establish connections with other neurons, and restore sensation and movement in the lower extremities.

2013

In 2013, I continued to make small improvements in therapy, and I wanted to make more trips. I enjoyed getting out of the house. In April of 2013, Christine and I took the Metro to opening day for the Nationals. It was my first-time riding Metro. Everything worked out fine and we had fun. In the future, I won't be taking Metro or attending opening day games anymore. It was too difficult getting around with the enormous crowds.

At Nat's Park with George and Christine

Then in May, Abu and I went to Ocean City, MD. I found a hotel on the boardwalk downtown. It had been at least 5 years since I had been there. Our family has had a beachfront condo for over 25 years. Growing up, we spent our summer vacations going to Ocean City. It was usually the highlight of my summers. There were many years when I went down to our condo once or twice a month. I would leave after work on Friday and come home Sunday afternoon. It seemed as soon as I had crossed the Chesapeake Bay Bridge, I left my troubles behind. I spent the morning on the deck as the sun rose and watched the sunset over the bay from Fager's island. Our place is on the top floor of a three-story walk-up. From 2004 to 2008, it was getting difficult climbing up those stairs. I dragged myself and bags up step by step. It was always worth it. Because as soon as I opened the sliding glass door and saw the ocean and smelled that "beach" smell, I felt immediately relaxed. There came a point when I just couldn't make the drive or make it up the stairs anymore. That was a huge loss for me.

Abu transferred me out of my power chair and in to the passenger seat and we headed off to the beach. As we drove over the Bay Bridge, I had the same calm feeling as usual and a few thoughts about all I had been through over the last year. I certainly wasn't where I wanted to be right now physically, but I felt good about the progress I had made in one year and I was excited to be heading to the beach. Abu wanted to stop at the Nike outlet store in Queenstown before a quick visit to see Christine in Easton. Christine moved to Easton many years ago to a beautiful house on the Miles river where she lives with her dog Sadie. I also hadn't been to her house in a long time. After our visit we drove on to Ocean City and got to the hotel Friday afternoon. We checked in and then headed out for a drive up coastal highway. It had been a few years since I had been there, and I wanted to see what things had changed. We drove up from our hotel on 13th street to our family's condo named the Pacesetter on 127th street. Marian had driven down from Delaware for the weekend to meet us. As Abu went up to see our unit, I rolled out into the parking lot and looked at our unit and the stairway that I had gone up and down hundreds of times. I was glad to be back. The three of us went to dinner at Fager's Island and we watched the sunset. On Saturday, we went down the legendary boardwalk and checked out the shops. Some of the shops and arcades have been there forever. We spent the afternoon sitting in the sun around the pool. We left on Sunday after breakfast and got home in the afternoon. It was my first trip away and it was successful. If I have Abu with me, we can go anywhere and over the next couple of years we did.

Valerie suggested to me one day in therapy that I should learn to drive my van. I could get the van equipped with the necessary hand controls, take driving lessons, and be on my way. At that time, that idea was crazy to me but as I've learned over the years there's no reason to argue with her. She's usually right. I went online and found an adaptive driving instructor in Richmond Virginia. John, the instructor, had a wheelchair van that had just about every adaptable piece of equipment you could think of. We met at my house and Abu drove me in my van to an empty parking lot nearby. I rolled in behind the wheel of John's van. I was extremely nervous. After describing my injury and my weaknesses, John said I would just need hand controls. I was familiar with hand controls because as my condition had deteriorated around 2010, I had them installed in my BMW. But instead of getting the necessary training, I drove out on the streets the day I got them and turning on a street near my house, I couldn't turn the wheel with one hand and crashed into two cars. This time I would do it the right way.

For my first lesson, I drove with John in the passenger seat, around the empty parking lot for about 30 minutes. I did well but was tired and mentally drained. Over the next 3 weeks, I took three more lessons starting out in the neighborhood and later driving around Vienna. I was driving better each time and getting more confident.

With my training completed, Abu and I took my van to a company in Greenbelt, Maryland. Not only were they going to install my hand controls, but also reconfigure the vans original drivers chair so that if needed, it could be locked back in place so that anyone could drive the van. Two weeks later, Christine and I took a taxi to pick up the van. After I checked to make sure everything was properly installed for me, we would put the driver's seat back in and Christine would drive it home because I wasn't licensed to drive the van yet.

There was only one problem, they never fixed the driver chair. Every time I called, I had reminded them to do it, but they didn't. There was only one way to get the van home and that was for me to drive it. Two other small issues, I had never driven my van and I had never driven on the beltway during my training. I locked my chair in behind the wheel and they loaded the useless driver's chair into the van. Christine got into the passenger seat, probably a little reluctantly, which I could understand. It was around 2:30 when I started the car. I've learned over the years to deal with certain difficult problems one small piece or task at a time. The idea of driving this van home on the beltway was a little intimidating. I figured I had about a half mile to drive and get used to the new hand controls before I got on route 1, then about 3 miles to the exit for the beltway. The next piece was the beltway and a drive about 15 miles to my exit on route 123 to Vienna. One thing I was worried about was I hadn't driven more than 25 miles an hour during my training. In the van neither one of us was talking. The radio was off. At the stoplights, I was taking deep breaths and gaining a tiny bit of confidence. I exited onto the beltway and got quickly into the right lane. I was doing 55 exactly which as anyone in the D.C. Metro area knows can get you killed. But that's my plan and it was working. Occasionally, I remembered to breathe, and we made it over the American Legion Bridge and then traffic slowed to a crawl. I was talking to myself saying, it's ok, we're almost there, you're doing great and soon we exited onto 123 towards Vienna and a couple of miles later I pulled safely onto my driveway. Both of us finally could exhale.

A few weeks went by and I was trying to find a company to adapt the driver's chair. I continued driving (unlicensed) to therapy and the store and a few other errands around Vienna and then a few weeks later, I very easily passed my Virginia driver's test. I did eventually get the chair fixed by a Ford dealership in Annapolis. I stored it in my porch and I never needed to use it. That trip from Greenbelt to Vienna had given me confidence and a new perspective of the future of my driving. When I initially decided to take driving lessons (thank you, Valerie, for the push) and get my hand controls, it was going to be for short trips, but now after conquering the beltway my world was going to get much bigger.

The rest of the summer I spent working out at therapy 3 times a week and going to a few Nationals games. One game, I decided to drive to Nationals Park by myself to see the Nats play. First, I was nervous. But my thought process was this: I knew I had driven to a few games already and I was successful. I just needed to break the trip into manageable pieces. Get in the van, make sure I had my parking pass and game ticket, and my bottle of water. I have enough gas, check. First step, leave early and drive to the park. That piece worked fine, although I can remember looking at myself in the rear-view mirror and thinking, what the hell are you doing? Always in the back of my mind was if at any time this didn't work, I would just turn around and go home. But it all worked out fine, no trouble, I stayed until the 7th inning and beat the traffic home. A complete success. For me, at that time in my continuing recovery, I was proud of myself. The funny thing about this trip is I would have never thought of making a trip like this by myself when I was physically better.

Late in the summer, Abu and I went to Christine's for a weekend. Her house is one level like mine and she had a ramp built so that I could get in. In the fall, some of my close college friends visited. I hadn't seen many of them in a couple of years. On Friday morning everyone got into my van and I drove us all to the National Air and Space Museum near Dulles Airport in Virginia. Everybody was really impressed with my driving after their nervousness wore off. The rest of the weekend we hung out at my house and had a great time catching up with each other. It was the start of future get togethers for our group. But the most important thing was my life was returning to normal.

2014

Looking back now, this was about the time when I was adjusting better to my new life. I was two years post-surgery and I began to think a little about my future. For a few years I was only able to deal with issues on a day to day basis, not thinking about what my future would look like. Putting out fires. Abu was coming every morning, as usual, and we had streamlined my morning: shower, toilet and dressing routine. In the evening, Diane and I had made my power chair to bed transfer relatively smooth. I was adjusting to my "new normal". Adjusting, but still not accepting. I was getting up at around 7:30 each morning, eating breakfast about 9 and going to therapy for a couple of hours. I could now focus on my rehab. I was home for lunch between 11:30 and 12. In the afternoon, I worked on my computer and watched some TV. After dinner, I would get into bed about 9 and read books on my kindle for a while, watch TV while playing some word games on my iPad. I would turn off the lights (using a remote light switch) about 11:30. That is pretty much my daily routine and sticking as close to that routine is the best way for me to have a good day.

The Spring and Summer weekends were spent with friends and family around the pool and evening cookouts. Bill and Jerry made visits and Shawn came up from Charlotte. Carole made a few trips from San Francisco. I really appreciate the efforts my out of town friends make to come and see me. I attended several Nationals games. All in all, a positive year.

As the year was ending, I was looking to try some new things. I was making small amounts of progress (which is important) at therapy but that my exercise routine, although effective, was getting a little repetitive. On the plus side, I wasn't having any additional physical problems, my pain and spasticity levels were the same but were manageable. As the year came to a close, I wanted to come up with some new challenges for the new year.

2015

In March, I took out a loan to get my master bathroom remodeled to make it easier for me to get into the room. My shower drain was leaking into my basement. My bathroom door frame was only 24" wide and I couldn't get my power chair through the door. My house is a 4-bedroom brick rambler built in 1955. I was unable to use the sink to wash my hands or brush my teeth. I had to do those things outside the bathroom. I used a shower chair that barely fit through the door. My friend Steve, who I first met while working at Reilly Mortgage, had started his own construction business. He found time to come down from Pennsylvania and in just over a week completely remodeled my entire bathroom. He made the shower a roll-in, with no curb and widened the door. It was a great job and gave me more independence. Now I can get in and out of my bathroom on my own. Some handicapped people must deal with a bathroom remodel or may need to install a stair lift to get upstairs to their bedroom. I point this out because of the extreme financial costs that come with certain medical issues. I'm lucky enough to have a one level home and so far, I have been able to afford the medical equipment and other handicapped items I need. I have also been able to take out loans to pay for my bathroom remodel and for the hand controls installation for my van. I can focus on my rehab and not worry about these issues. But I will need to deal with these issues for the rest of my life. There are many people who are not as fortunate. They are fighting many financial and health battles and it can get overwhelming. It's just something to think about if you have a friend or relative dealing with a long-term medical issue and it's something you should personally keep in mind for yourself as you get older. If you are currently in good health, don't take it for granted. Watch what you are eating and start an exercise plan if you're not working out already. Get an annual physical, have your blood pressure checked. I know you've heard all of this before but as you get older it's even more important for you and your family. I hope that you will continue to be healthy and not have to deal with any health issues for many years. I would give anything to be able to take a few steps on my own. Go for a walk. I am jealous of you all that you can do it. Exercise now and 15 to 20 years from now you'll be glad you did. If you feel like I'm guilt tripping you, well, I guess I am.

In early Spring, I was researching the possibility of taking a cruise. I had taken my first and only cruise in 2000 with many friends of mine that were celebrating our 40th birthdays on a trip to the Caribbean. The ships today are well equipped for handicapped persons. I made a few calls to my friends to see if they had any interest in taking a 7-day cruise out of Baltimore Harbor to Bermuda. In the end my friend Tom Looney (Tom's wife Trish had a last-minute family emergency) Abu and I took the trip.

In early June, I drove to the Baltimore Harbor with Abu. We parked the van and dropped off our bags. After getting settled in our room, we met Tom on the main deck of the Royal Caribbean's Grandeur of the Seas for the departure party, and soon were sailing under the Bay Bridge, out into the Atlantic, and on our way to Bermuda. My handicapped room worked well, and I was able to get everywhere on the ship. The food was amazing, and we saw shows every evening. Tom and I spent late evenings either in the casino or the clubs while Abu went out on his own. In Bermuda, the three of us toured the Royal Navy Dockyard, the town where the ship had docked. We stayed in Bermuda for two days before returning to Baltimore. We had a great time and we plan to do another cruise in the next few years hopefully with a few more people.

Bermuda Cruise with Tom Looney and Abu

In the Spring and Summer, I continued to make small improvements at therapy and any improvements, are positive. I was no longer taking my blood pressure medication and because of my workouts, there were very few mornings that I felt lightheaded. My therapy consisted of standing or taking a few assisted steps in the parallel bars, riding a stationary hand and arm bike, lifting free weights and doing some hand exercises. My strength and stamina were increasing. APT has many different pieces of equipment so I can change my routine. As Valerie's business grew, she asked Abu to work at APT. Since 2012, when Abu started working with me in the mornings, he would always go with me to therapy to help me with my workout. Eventually, he was lending a hand to other patients and Valerie saw what a caring person he is. He likes helping people and is dedicated to his work.

Valerie is always thinking about new therapies, new ways of getting the maximum improvement for her patients. She is constantly searching the internet for cutting edge robotic equipment. She has a large group of fellow neurological therapists and doctors dedicated to helping patients, like myself, to achieve our best physical outcomes. As a Doctor of Physical

Therapy, and as someone at the forefront of her field, she is asked to speak at conferences around the world. In the fall of 2015, I attended a Working 2 Walk Symposium held in Bethesda, Maryland. The annual conference is held in major cities around the country and the top spinal cord researchers and scientists from around the world come to share their research and update the attendees. Some of the sessions included:

The importance of clinical trials, Neural networks leading to epidural stimulation, Neural Networks, The Miami project Schwann Cell clinical trials and What is the cure? I hadn't researched any of these topics before the conference and that was something I should have done before I went. Listening to the speakers gave me hope that there were groups in the United States and around the world, dedicated to finding a cure for spinal cord injuries. It was a little disappointing that these potential cures were years away from being tested on injured patients. They explained the role of the FDA and how much funding these efforts needed. It was an eye opening two days but all in all very positive. Where some research had shown animals recovering from paralysis through treatment the same treatment was not approved for humans.

Ekso Robotic: Eksoskeleton

Meanwhile, Valerie was setting up multiple demos of robotic walking devices at APT. One device was called ReWalk. ReWalk is a wearable robotic exoskeleton that provides powered hip and knee motion to enable individuals with spinal cord injury (SCI) to stand upright, walk, turn, and climb and descend stairs. Another vendor with a slightly different product was Indego. Indego® is a powered lower limb exoskeleton enabling people with spinal cord injuries to walk and participate in over ground gait training. But the one that Valerie found to be the most beneficial for her patients was the Ekso Bionics Eksoskeleton. The company demonstrated the device at APT with a T-10 injured employee. He sat in a chair and the Ekso was fitted to his legs and then a torso wrap, and a backpack that contained the batteries and controller. He activated the Ekso suit and following a beep he stood up from the chair. He pushed another button, then a beep and he started to slowly take steps. He was using forearm crutches to help with shifting left and right and with balance. He walked around the PT facility for 15 minutes and sat down in the chair where he started.

I wanted an opportunity to try it but as I later learned you first must get a doctor's prescription and then be evaluated by a therapist. You also must be able to bear weight on your legs and have a certain amount of flexibility in your legs. Valerie knew how much I wanted to try Ekso and finally in mid-October I got my chance when the company brought the robotic device back to APT. Dr. Sheehan wrote me a prescription to use the Ekso. It took about 15 minutes for Valerie to get accurate measurements of my upper and lower legs. The Ekso is fully customizable for each patient. The Ekso was placed in a chair and Abu transferred me to the chair holding the device. Then the legs were fastened with Velcro straps around my feet, calves and thighs. The abdomen wrap was secured, and the backpack straps were tightened around my shoulders. I was sitting in the chair, excited and nervous. I was hoping I would be able to walk but I wasn't sure. There were at least 15 people watching. I had a walker in front of me being held by Abu. The Ekso technician was operating the controller showing Valerie the different walking settings. She pushed a button to stand and with a little help from Carlos, I was standing in the Ekso. The best way to describe it is it's like a frame or scaffold. I was ready to take my first step. I was set up in the "manual mode" where Valerie would trigger each step I took. I shifted slightly to the left and I stepped with my right leg. I was bearing full weight on my legs, but the robot was lifting my leg and helping me step forward. I was visualizing the step in my head, but the robot was fully assisting me. I shifted right and "beep" my left leg steps. I was keeping my balance and shifting with the walker. Left step, right step, left step, right step. It had been over three and a half years but finally I was walking again. It felt great to be standing up and walking. It was taking all my physical effort and complete concentration. I walked a few more steps and I was finished. The chair was moved behind me and one more beep and I was sitting. I was exhausted but really happy. The Ekso was taken off me and I was transferred back to my power chair. This device has a lot of potential for me and Valerie's patients but it's very expensive. But I've got to find a way to get back in that Ekso.

Leave it to Valerie to find a way to get the Ekso into her practice. I wouldn't be surprised if she mortgaged her house. She's that committed to us. She and her staff, Carlos and Abu, had to be certified to operate the Ekso robot. That took over 40 hours of training. Valerie gave me the opportunity to be one of the Ekso training patients, so they can get their certifications. I would come for an hour or two 4 days in a row. If I was honest, I wasn't sure I was physically ready to do that, but I was keeping that to myself.

It was Monday morning December 7th, and most of my mornings were normal, no physical issues, but there were a few days a month when my blood pressure was very low. I've stated that my bp runs usually 82/60, but on that morning, I was probably 65/50 - yes, that low. Sometimes it's the weather, sometimes I have nights where I pee almost every hour and that can make me dehydrated. I couldn't worry about the cause that morning, it was my scheduled time to help with the training. After getting secured in the robot, I was taking deep breaths and sips of water. The person (in this case Valerie) said the command "hold for stand" she pressed the button on the remote and I stood up with help from Abu. The trainer from the company, Chantel, was going over the different features and settings with Carlos, Valerie and Abu while I'm standing. I was doing ok. Time to walk. In my case Valerie triggered each step when I was in the proper position. There was some talk between each step, and I was getting tired. I took 14 steps and I needed to stop. I was tired, out of breath, stressed and getting hot. I was only on my feet for about 10 minutes. It was disappointing to me to have such a short walk. Valerie was giving me words of encouragement because she could see how disappointed I was. As the guys took me out of the Ekso, I heard the trainer say to Valerie that I might not be a viable candidate to continue the training for the rest of the week. I understood her thinking because they needed someone that could stand and walk for at least 15 to 20 minutes. But hearing her say that made me mad but not at her. The next day would be different.

On Tuesday, my training time was scheduled for later in the morning. There were five training patients that were working with Valerie, Carlos and Abu. Each of us had a different kind of disability. That gave them different challenges and they would be able to learn how to adjust the Ekso to maximize each patient's walking. I was back in the Ekso at noon and I was feeling much better. I had more energy and I was less nervous, and I had a big chip on my shoulder from the previous days' poor performance. At the end of my second session, I had been up almost twenty minutes and had walked 147 steps, and best of all the training was helpful. I still had the competitor in me. The rest of that week's training went well, and Valerie, Carlos and Abu earned their certifications. As 2015 ended, I was looking forward to working more with the Ekso and eagerly anticipating Valerie's new therapy program for me.

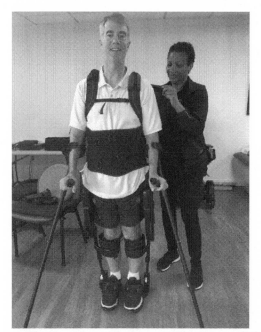

Ready to walk in the Esko robot, with Valerie

2016

I hadn't planned any trips for the year and on a positive note, I didn't have any additional physical issues. 2016 was another good year. I was eager to get working on my new therapy plan which included sessions walking in the Ekso robot and riding a new piece of equipment the RT300. Early in 2016, Valerie purchased a FES bike. The Functional Electronic Stimulation (FES) is the application of electrical impulses to paralyzed muscles causing a series of contractions and relaxations creating a functional movement, riding a bike. The electrical impulses are applied to the leg muscles via electrodes on the skin above the muscles. Studies showed improvements to neurological and some functional gains, as well as enhanced physical health demonstrated by decreased fat and increased muscle mass. I was walking in the robot once or twice a week and riding the FES bike once a week. I was also working on strengthening my arms, hands and core using other exercise equipment. By mid-year, I was averaging 250 steps in the robot per sessions. A big improvement from the 14 steps I took on my first walk at the end of 2015.

When you first see someone walking in the robot you might think its primary purpose is to get them walking again. I thought so too but the first significant thing that happened for me was an increase in stamina. I was walking more steps, but I wasn't completely exhausted when I stopped. Because of my improvement, Valerie was no longer triggering each step, I was doing it myself by being in the correct position and now I had only 1 tech helping me. The next thing I noticed was my afternoon was almost pain free. The walking loosened my joints, got my blood circulating and helped with the fluid buildup in my legs due to sitting in the wheelchair all day. My blood pressure was a little higher and I wasn't light headed in the morning when I first woke up. And then there's the mental part. I didn't realize how much being able to walk in the robot would positively affect my outlook on the future of my recovery. It gives you hope and that's what we as patients desperately want and need. I see that happen every single time a new patient stands up in the Ekso and walks across the room, when in some cases they haven't stood for many years. The patient is crying, their family is crying, oh hell, everybody in the room is crying. It never gets old.

I worked hard the rest of the year, getting stronger, increasing my steps and building muscles. I am trying to keep my bones and muscles strong. When the scientists and researchers find a cure to bridge my damaged nerve area, I need to be able to have strong legs to support my body weight. Brittle bones and atrophied muscles won't work. Riding the FES bike, standing in the parallel bars and walking in the robot will help me maintain my strength.

I know that when I try to move my leg, my brain sends a signal to my leg that right now is getting blocked by the damage to my spinal cord. It's the same signal that was sent to those 15-year-old legs that ran up and down basketball courts and football fields. My legs are just waiting for the signal to get there. It's so simple, I just need a bridge or bypass around the damage. It's going to happen and when it does, I want to make sure my bones are strong, and my muscles are stronger. Just flip the switch and turn the power back on and I'll get up out of this damn wheelchair and walk again!

In the late Spring of 2016, our group of friends, mostly Mount grads, got together again in Ocean City for a weekend of golf and catching up. My friend Jeff has a beautiful condo in a building with an elevator. A few guys stayed with me and the rest stayed at our family's condo. It's great to get together with everyone.

Ocean City - Rick Spenser, Jerry Sgrignoli, Tom Castaldi, Pete Monahan, Tom Brown

As all of you pet owners know, at some point you will have to say goodbye to your loyal friend. For Diane and me and all the Brown family, that came in May. Boomer, 14 years old, had been struggling with weakness in his back legs for many months and had also developed a tumor in his nose. He was probably struggling with it for a little while, but he never showed it. He was slower, and he slept a lot but still loved laying by the pool and going for walks and, of course, he loved his treats. Late one evening, Diane noticed Boomer was bleeding profusely from his nose and she took him to the emergency vet. The next day we made the tough but humane decision that many pet owners make. He was a great dog; a loyal friend and we still miss him especially when I open the pool in the Spring. He loved to swim.

In mid-June, Diane, Christine and I went to a Nationals game. I was going to 6 or 7 games each season. We were leaving after the game and getting into my van when the side door where my ramp is, got stuck and wouldn't open all the way. I eventually found out that the cable attached to the motor that opens the door had broken and got jammed in the wheels of the door. The door would not open with the key remote but after getting help from another fan we were able to get the door opened enough for me to get in, but the door wouldn't shut tight. Christine had to hold the door shut all the way home from downtown DC. The van didn't have that many miles on it, but it was 9 years old. I knew my rear shocks needed to be replaced and I needed new brakes and the check engine light was coming on every so often. To get the door fixed was well over $1,000. The final straw came one morning on my way to therapy. I started the car, but I couldn't pull the gear shift down from park to drive. It was stuck. Abu tried to pull it down and he pulled the stuck handle so hard he broke it in half. The car went into reverse and was rolling into the neighbor's yard. He shut off the car and I had to have the van towed to the gas station. I had them make the car drivable and with the side door closed with bungee cords. After getting expensive quotes to repair it, I ended up trading it for a new van.

It was about that same time that I was having the van trouble that I was asked to join a startup company based in McLean, Virginia. The company is called Phoenix Innovations and we create, design and develop products that help in physical and neurological therapy practices. We are currently developing a few products that will help patients with spasticity and improve patients walking. Initially I was hesitant to take the job because I didn't want to commit to the position and then due to any number of reasons, not be able to contribute in a positive way or work every day. But I agreed to join the company, and everything has worked out fine. Since this second injury, I sometimes worry about or over analyze things. It has been 10 years since I've worked, but the two years has been very rewarding to be involved with this group of people who are dedicated and have a true passion for helping. Our team is always looking for any way to improve or enhance existing products or in most cases, design and develop our own ideas. We knew this would be tough and take some time, but our owner is a successful entrepreneur who shares the same vision we all do.

Four months after Boomer was gone, Diane started to look through the internet for rescue dogs. She searched for a while knowing she wanted another Lab. She located a female yellow lab in a shelter in South Carolina through a rescue group called Lucky Dog Animal Rescue (LDAR). Suzy has worked with Lucky Dog for many years. She fosters and then places the puppies in homes around the area. After filling out forms and waiting a few days, two-year-old Daisy (formerly Phoebe) was driven up to Virginia where Diane and Katy picked her up and brought her home. She has turned out to be a great dog. She quickly learned to swim and likes to play with her cousin Sadie, who Christine adopted from a shelter 8 years ago and Belle and Riley who were also shelter dogs and live with Tom and Suzy.

Daisy

2017

In March, our Mount group planned another get together. For the last two years most of our core group of friends had met every six months or so usually close to the D.C. area because it's somewhat central to everyone and because it's a little easier for me to attend. This year we decided to meet in Tom Looney's town of Wilmington, NC for a weekend to watch college basketball and to find out what everyone had been up to. Tom and his wife Trish, hosted me, Abu, Bill (chairman) Pete Monahan (Tom's college roommate) and Shawn. Bill came down from Scranton and drove me and Abu to Wilmington. That drive is too long for me to make on my own. We installed the van's drivers chair and I sat in my chair in the middle of the van. After a 7-hour drive, we arrived Friday afternoon and Abu and I checked into the hotel. That evening we all met in a sports bar for dinner. For lunch on Saturday, we got together at an oceanfront restaurant near the Looney's beach house. We ate and drank and retold stories from our college days, with some embellishments. Even though we all live apart from each other, when we get together it's like we are back together at the Mount. For dinner,

Tom and Trish reserved the clubhouse in their neighborhood where we watched the college basketball tournament in the theatre room and Trish cooked an amazing gourmet meal for us and some local friends and family. On Sunday, we packed up and made the trip home. I know with everyone's busy home and work schedules it's not easy to make these trips but as we get a little older everyone knows how important our get togethers are. We also made plans for our upcoming 35th class reunion.

Tom Looney, Bill "Chairman" Young, Shawn Fennell and Pete Monahan

In June, the Mount St. Mary's class of 1982 had our 35th reunion. I decided to go for the day. For me to stay overnight anywhere requires Abu to come with me as well as bringing many other things I need, so a day trip was my best option. I hadn't been to a college class reunion in many years and I had gotten a few calls from close friends that they were going to go. Time for another adventure.

I drove up to the Mount Friday morning and I got there at noon. I have to say I am always a little hesitant to attend these reunions or any group get together in a wheelchair. When I roll into a room of people, I feel like I am a focal point whereas I just want to blend in. Maybe I shouldn't care, but I do. As time goes on, I am getting better dealing with it. I don't have a choice because there's still a lot of things I want to do.

I met up with Tom and Trish Looney. Soon after I arrived, Tom went to visit the Mount's long-time basketball coach Jim Phelan. I told Tom I would pick him up at 2 o'clock. I took a drive around the campus to see the many improvements since I'd last been there. I drove a mile down the road from campus to the Phelan's house to get Tom. Dottie, the coach's wife, was in the driveway when I pulled in and asked me to come in and say hi to coach Phelan. What I figured would be a quick hello, turned into an hour of reminiscing with Tom, Dottie and Coach. I hadn't seen coach Phelan in over 10 years since the 1981 basketball team was honored at halftime of a men's basketball game. As the public address announcer, I was asked to join members of the team at half court during the halftime of a Men's basketball game. I was honored to be included.

I knew that coach was going through some recent health challenges leading up to the reunion weekend, but he looked great. Their home was full of family pictures and the family room where we all met had many pictures and mementos of past Mount teams. Many tributes to coach Phelan and awards scattered all over the shelves. But the most memorable part of the visit was reliving the games and talking about the players, and how coach Phelan gave behind the scenes insight into plays and last-second victories. Tom would bring up a big game and Coach would relate a behind the scenes story that not many knew. It was amazing. If I could have gotten ESPN cameras in there it would have been an incredible show. I think we could have reminisced for hours, but Tom and I needed to get back to campus. Before we left, Dottie, whose memory of games and players is remarkable to me, took me into their living room to show me a beautiful painted portrait of coach Phelan wearing his signature bow tie and then his college basketball hall of fame medal. On the way back to the family room, she showed me a window in their kitchen with shelves covered with pictures of their children and grandchildren. Then she proudly said "These are my trophies "

It was time to leave and I said goodbye to Coach and walked out of the house with Dottie onto the driveway leaving Tom behind with coach Phelan. Tom called out to us to wait that Coach wanted to see my van and to say goodbye. Dottie seemed pleasantly surprised that he wanted to come outside. The whole time we talked Coach was sitting in his recliner with his walker next to him. I wasn't sure about his mobility, but he was out on the driveway walking just fine. My van was 20 feet away and as I was making my way to the van, Tom was saying his goodbyes and coach said loudly, "you're my hero." I assumed he was talking to Tom, but Tom said to me, "did you hear Coach?, he said you're his hero." I waved and said thanks and as we drove back to campus, I was speechless. It was the highlight of the day.

Shawn had planned to visit his sisters in early July and on Monday, July 3rd, we went out to lunch to quietly celebrate our 40th anniversary. For many years, right after my diving accident, we would celebrate the 4th in a bar with friends and usually be hungover the next morning. One celebratory shot at

11:30 pm would lead to another and another. This time our lunch at the Tower Oaks in Rockville, MD was much more subdued. We had a lot to be proud of like Shawn's family, his wife Lisa and wonderful children Bryan and Allie. Since Shawn and his family now live in Charlotte, NC we don't get together as much as we would like to, but we text and talk weekly and see each other usually once a year.

It had been 5 years since I got my original power chair. My health insurance plan allows me to receive a new power chair every 5 years. I must pay 20% deductible. It's a good thing because my current chair was having some issues. Today's chairs have better features, more seating positions, better cushions, and wheel suspensions to make the ride smoother. My new chair is designed so that I can stand up in it. I have a leg piece that blocks my knees and a metal bar, placed in front of my chest, that stops me from falling forward. I'm excited about this feature because now I can stand up on my own anytime I want to. Prior to getting the new chair, I could only stand when I was at therapy and with the help of a therapy tech. I know that standing more frequently and for a longer duration, will help strengthen my bones and muscles and will help me with my walking and my overall health.

Lessons I've learned

Here are a few things I've learned so far over the many years dealing with the challenges in my life. They are coping tools I've used to give me the best chance to lead a happy, successful, and meaningful life. I've learned like most people, by trying and failing many times. Usually trying to fix, adjust to, or get around an issue I've had to confront. They are in no order or importance.

Have a Routine

I've mentioned that I operate best when I stick to a routine. Going to bed and waking up at the same time gives me the best chance to have a successful day. I watch what I eat because for me, having weight issues can make my rehab more difficult and having limited mobility (wheelchair bound) makes it harder to burn calories and keep my weight down. I also don't want to be too rigid in my routine because that might inhibit me from going out at night or traveling or meeting with friends. I try to have a balance.

Exercise/Therapy

Most mornings you can find me at therapy. Primarily, I am there to work out, but it's turned out to be a lot more than an exercise facility. I've been going there for almost 10 years now. I have met many people at APT who have become my friends. We all have challenges that we are dealing with, and we are all working hard to get better. We have a common goal, to maximize our physical potential. There are some people I have known and worked besides, for many years and some others I have known for just a couple of months, but we have bonded quickly. We have a small group of people, which I refer to as the APT unofficial board of directors, that meet for lunch once a month. It's an interesting visual at the restaurant where we have 3 or 4 wheelchairs, a scooter and a walker or two, but we have a great time and I hope will continue. There is a degree of comfort being around people who have common struggles. We are loud and laugh a lot.

Like I said, I have been going to therapy on a regular basis. It's now part of my routine. I have gotten to the point that if I don't exercise for 2 or 3 days in a row my pain increases and my spasticity gets worse and I generally don't feel good. For me, working out isn't a choice anymore and because I have worked so hard for many years, I feel like I'm in the best shape physically now than I've been for at least 10 years.

Pain Management

A lot of people have pain and for some it's chronic. I have what's called neuropathic pain from my injury in 1977. It was exacerbated by my surgery in 2012. Neuropathic pain is often described as a shooting or burning pain. It can go away on its own but is often chronic. Sometimes it is unrelenting and severe, and sometimes it comes and goes. It often is the result of nerve damage or a malfunctioning nervous system. The impact of nerve damage is a change in nerve function both at the site of the injury and areas around it. Today, most of my chronic pain is in my legs and feet and it is worst in the late afternoon and evening. It's mostly a dull aching pain in my knees and hips and moderate to severe burning pain in my feet. A few days a week it will be a sharp stabbing pain and it wakes me up when I'm sleeping. I do some form of exercise 5 days a week now and that helps with the pain and spasticity. Also, due to the nerve damage, I can't regulate my body temperature. I am usually feeling cold. It's weird because I can't tell the difference between cold and hot water on my skin below my neck. I am cold in the summer, because of air conditioning and cold in the winter because, you know, it's winter. I'm always trying to get warm, and anytime I can sit in the sun, I feel better though I must to be careful in the heat because I don't sweat, and I can get overheated quickly.

Another thing that helps with my pain is to find a distraction. If I'm out somewhere with friends, at dinner, a movie or a ballgame, I'm less likely to think about my pain then if I was by myself at home watching TV. I do use prescription pain medication, but it's always a last resort. For me, it can help lower the severity of the pain, but it never fully relieves it. I take some over the counter medication after a tough workout to get ahead of the pain before it gets bad. Using ice for me works better than heat. Once extreme pain settles in it's more difficult to get relief. I have recently started using CBD oil and medical marijuana and I have gotten relief from pain and spasticity. I track my pain levels almost daily and the factors that may have caused it. Did I overdo at therapy? Is it the weather? Did I not sleep well? I try to find correlations between my pain and outside factors so I'm more prepared to deal with it. I've had many years fighting my pain and there are many combinations to try. I haven't figured it out yet but I'm always working on it.

Focus on the Positive

I've been trying to find a reason that I've had to deal with all these challenges. Is there some greater plan at work or am I just a random victim of bad luck? For many years right after my injury, I was waiting for some lightbulb moment, where I would find myself in a situation and say, "this is why I got injured and recovered." But that never happened and as many years passed, I stopped looking for a reason. Then just in the last year or so I've gotten such satisfaction from spending time with the people or other random victims of bad luck who must deal with challenges of their own. There are people dealing with unexpected strokes, Parkinson's or MS and young men and women with spinal cord injuries. I get energized working, struggling, laughing and crying alongside these wonderful individuals who don't deserve to be in this predicament any more than I do. I share with them any ideas from my experience that might help them. It's starting to make sense that this is where I belong right now. I'm inspired watching a new patient come into therapy sometimes scared, tired and quiet, and then watch them after working hard for weeks get out of their wheelchairs and talk to everyone and smile. The main reason this is happening is Valerie

Gibson. Over the 9 plus years that I've known her, she has worked tirelessly to get her patient's the best equipment, best therapy plans and best chance at maximizing their potential. In the time I've been there I've seen many patients (I don't like the word patient but can't think of another word) make significant improvements. They've shared stories of spending years at other PT facilities and how much better they've done in just a couple of months at APT. Valerie tries different therapies, exercises that she feels will help, tremendous out of the box therapeutic treatments. She has new ideas for us on any given day when we come through the door of her therapy center and if you're smart you listen, and you try her idea. But you must have a positive attitude and that's not always easy when you're facing a life altering injury or disease.

When you find yourself in a situation like that, take time to process what has happened, but not too much time. Then make a plan and ask for help if you are struggling. Do your best to get accurate information on your ailment. Doctors don't know everything. One of the most important pieces of the plan must be step 1. Decide to fight, to get better. Get up out of your chair. Get out of the house. Change the scenery. Because you will encounter speed bumps and dead ends during your recovery. I've encountered all kinds of problems and the only thing you can do is to keep trying. I haven't found any other good option. I'm definitely not going to sit in my house anymore and do nothing and as I have written I've had good reasons to just quit. I will tell you that there are days when I take a day off, physically and/or mentally. Using a sports metaphor, I'll call a timeout. Nobody can be "on their game" every day. If you're having a bad day or two, don't worry, just take time for yourself and be ready to go tomorrow or the next day. But don't give up, just try to do your best.

This is a scenario that many people face for any number of reasons. It's a critical juncture where you must make a decision to fight or not. To fight against the ease of staying at home. Doing this might lead to a downward spiraling effect where your predicament gets worse or you can decide to put one foot in front of the other and attack your problem. Find any reason to get out of the house, go have lunch with a friend or go for a walk with your dog. Anything but staying at home and if that is too hard, talk to a friend or family member that will give you a nudge or even a push to get you moving in the right direction.

My Perspective

I feel like I'm walking a tightrope some days, but I have a lot of experience up there. I must be very careful not to get sick. If I get the flu, a stomach bug, a respiratory infection or pneumonia, it could be very bad for me. I also must be careful of pressure sores. I've had my problems with them in the past and they can happen quickly. Any one of these issues can really knock me out for a long period of time. I worry about my wheelchair breaking or if something would happen to Abu. I am trying to have backup plans, but I can't plan for every scenario and worrying about it too much isn't good. I spend a lot of time trying to put myself in a position for success. The best thing for me to do is enjoy each day and if I'm faced with an issue, use all my resources to deal with it. As my mother used to say, "don't borrow trouble." I've been able to focus on the positive, which is difficult, and not worry about what I don't have. I can't walk right now but I'm going out to shows and ball games and spending time with family and friends. I'm enjoying my life the best I can. The clock is ticking. All in all, I feel that I've done a pretty good job dealing with everything, so far.

I've never accepted my injury. I have always thought of my situation as rehabbing from an injury. I've never felt like my current condition was permanent. I still see small improvements in my hands, legs and stamina. My standing and walking are improving and as long as this continues, I am content. This latest setback is just taking longer to recover. I am constantly adapting, trying to make my daily life easier using adaptive products. I search the internet for products or think them up in the middle of the night. These new ideas can be worked on with the help of Phoenix Innovations. I'll do this until I'm up and walking. I don't see any other option. I also want to be physically ready when there is a medical breakthrough in spinal cord research so that I can be a preferred candidate to be selected for the clinical trial or treatment.

I know now that just because I've had all these struggles it doesn't exempt me from another major challenge, injury or illness. I'm doing my best to stay in the best shape I can and to be ready for the next fight. Like I said, I believe that was a big factor in my recovery from my diving accident. I'm trying to do something that I'm pretty sure not too many people (if any) have ever done, make a full recovery from being totally paralyzed twice. It's the challenge that keeps me going. The athlete is still in there.

I figure I'll finish this book now with my life in a good place. I'm healthy, I'm working again and still making progress at therapy. Someone once wrote: you measure progress in inches, especially when you don't have yards or even feet of success to show off. My legs aren't working yet but the way they responded after my first paralysis was amazing, so I'm ok with that, for now. I'll be seeing my friends a couple of times this year, attending several Nats games and hopefully a few concerts. I'll spend time with my friends, family and dogs around the pool at Beulah Beach and get back to the beach once or twice. Of course, there will be lunches with the APT "board" and lunches with my Uncle Chick. As I've said, Shali and Jeff live close by and I see them frequently and Carole and I will see movies and concerts as much as possible. I have a lot to look forward to this year and many years in the future. It took a lot of hard work on my part and help from many friends and of course my great family to get to where I am today and I'm going to enjoy this time, this third chance, if I'm able. I can't change the past decisions and I'm not worrying too much about the future. I'm just doing the best that I can today.

I'll finish with one short story. A couple of years ago, one of my friends and longtime therapy goers, Debbie, was listening to me respond to someone who had asked what had happened to me. It takes a few minutes to tell my story (as you now know) so that a person can understand my situation. A few minutes later she came over to me and said, "How do you do it?" "How do you deal with all you've been through and still have a positive attitude?" At the time, I told her that I have no idea, maybe I'm just crazy. The things I've dealt with throughout the years and now what I must deal with every day, I guess I would have every reason to be beaten down and just give in. I really have never thought about it. But after writing this book, I think I may have figured out an answer to Debbie's question. It's the many people that have helped me in the past and those people that help me every day. It's a group effort, my support system, and without this group no matter how much effort I give or how hard I try, I would never have gotten to where I am today without them, and THAT, is basically how I do it.

I feel, that inside every person, is the ability to overcome adversities they face in their life. They just have to find it within themselves or maybe remember my mother's words, that night that she said to an exhausted, scared, 17-year-old boy lying in intensive care, "I know you can do it."

Acknowledgements

I want to thank Karen Lawrence for suggesting that I write this book and Valerie Gibson for seconding the motion. Spending time with them and relating many stories over the years about my "adventures" led them to encourage me to write a book. I had stories but didn't think I had enough for a book. After their persistence, I finally gave it a try and I'm really glad I did. I started with my initial accident on the 4th of July and after writing almost every night for over a year and a half I finished it. It was Karen's email to me that my book would help or even inspire people that finally got me started and both Valerie and Karen's encouragement throughout the writing process that kept me going. I told very few people what I was doing because I wasn't sure I would finish it, but I did. Thanks to the people who gave me important feedback during early versions of the book. I wrote as I remembered but that wasn't always accurate, and their suggestions helped me fill in some missing pieces. Thanks to Karen for her editing and suggestions along the way and to Maggie Peacock for her help with the final edits that got me to the finish line.

I would like to acknowledge the caregivers. The husbands, wives, sons, daughters, siblings and friends. You have found yourselves in a situation that you obviously weren't expecting to be in but then neither was your loved one. From my perspective, when you are face to face with a life changing accident or diagnosis you may feel alone and maybe backed into a corner, thinking there is no way out. You don't want to be a burden and you are crushed. You can't believe this has happened to you. It's at that critical time that you need a helping hand from someone, and you, the caregiver are there. You take on this new role, possibly untrained and not ready, but you do everything you can to help your loved one. Thank you.

For those who have chosen, as a career, to be a helper, thank you. I see you doing this service, not as a job, but as a calling. You physically help your clients daily and offer words of encouragement along the way when we are struggling or having a bad day. You are there for us when we are at our lowest point. You are all special people and we would not have a chance to lead a normal life if you weren't there for us. For me that's Abu, my helper, my friend and now a family member. I start 99.9% of my days with Abu opening my bedroom door at 8 am. He has come every day for 6 years, rain or shine, healthy or sick and in case of snow, he stays overnight to make sure I'm up, showered and dressed. He has answered my emergency calls more than a few times and raced back to help me. We have had some fun trips together and he gets along with all my friends and family. I am very lucky to have him in my corner and I hope our partnership continues for many more years.

I want to acknowledge my fellow friends at APT. Some of you I have known for years and some of you I have only known for a short time. You all inspire me every day. You have decided that you are not going to accept your predicament. You have shown me your strength and courage and that makes me want to continue my fight every day. We work hard, encourage and sometimes make fun of each other and just as important we laugh together each morning. And then there are the monthly lunches. When we descend upon a local restaurant with big power chairs, wheelchairs, scooters and walkers. What a picture we paint. I hope the other patrons see us the way we are, tough resourceful proud men and women, just enjoying life. We certainly didn't sign up for this, but you all have faced your adversities with determination, toughness and at times, laughter. You have pushed me to get better when I needed it and your words of encouragement are most welcomed. I'm looking forward to continuing our fight.

So, thank you Debbie G. (Ibrahim) Nate, Angela, Claudia, Mike, Mary Beth, TJ (Joseph), Doris, Ev, Diane (Dick) , Terry, Kathleen (Pam),   David, Ken, Wesley, Bob, Barbara, Mary Alice, Roy, Daniel, Karen, Mary Ellen, Debbie, Frank, Roseann (Sal),   Evelyn, Roxanna, Jim, Sukla, Tapan, Joan, Jesse, Felix, Ben, Donna, Arlene (Mary), Bob, Tuan (Kim Anh), Rosie, Sinead, Jose, Adam, Mary, and Shirley. I'm sure I've forgotten others.

Family

Where to start. I've referenced the help and support my family has given me at many times throughout this book. Not just Tom and Suzy, Christine, Marian and Diane but my nieces and nephew. Also, my Uncle Chick, who I have been lucky enough to spend time with over the last few years at our wonderful lunches. At 93, he has demonstrated to our family how to live a good life. He served his country in the Navy and was our family's dentist. My Magner cousins, Meg, Claire and her husband Mark and Pat and his wife Margaret have supported me over many years. My Aunts, Sally and Sue, and all my Brown cousins, spouses and children that have followed my progress and offered encouraging messages and some who have been nice to visit me when they were in town.

Obviously, none of this would have been possible without my Mother and Dad. They're not with us anymore, but I feel their support for me when I need it.

Friends

Thanks to my friends, too many to name, who have helped me over the last forty years. Some of you who have literally picked me up off the ground and carried me physically and all who listened to me and offered words of encouragement when they were needed most. You have all been an important part of my much-needed support system.

APT

Advanced Physical Therapy has been my rock. I start most of my mornings there but there are some days that I don't feel like going. Rain, freezing weather, or just generally feeling bad or tired would be an acceptable excuse for staying home. But I don't. I figure doing any physical activity is better than staying home. I've done some of my best work there when I was feeling terrible. I also don't want to let people down who have given me the chance to recover from my injuries. I want to thank Valerie and her therapists Christine, Kathryn and Nowell, and therapy techs Carlos, Abu, Bryant and Katie at APT for helping me get better every day.

Thanks to all of you. My incredible support system. I am very lucky to have you all in my life. I will see you all very soon I hope and to the gang at APT, I'll see you tomorrow!

Success consists of going from failure to failure without loss of enthusiasm
- Anonymous

Me

My Mother with Shawn at my wedding

Uncle JB, Cousin Jay, Cousin Pat, Uncle Chick

My Family

Me and Abe

Pete, Tom, Me, Shawn, Billy